A Very Thin Line:

My Journey with Bipolar

———————

a memoir

Rohan Sharma
"Rx Mundi"

Rhythm & Bones Press
Trauma-turned-Art

Rhythm & Bones Press
Birdsboro, Pennsylvania

A Very Thin Line: My Journey with Bipolar
© 2019 Rohan Sharma, Rx Mundi, LLC
© 2019 Rhythm & Bones Press

Interior & Cover Design: Tianna G. Hansen
ISBN: 978-0-9980432-1-0
First Edition November 2019

www.rhythmnbone.com/a-very-thin-line

Content warning: This work deals with some difficult subjects including graphic depictions of self-harm, mental illness and some moments of violence. Take care while reading.

Advanced Praise for *A Very Thin Line*

"Sharma's informal and conversational writing style makes for a fast-paced read and paints a vivid picture as if he's sitting right beside you, telling you his story in person.

There have been many impressive memoirs about mental health. Very few, however, take those memoirs and add an extra layer of the confinement of prison.

Under that context, it wouldn't be wrong to say that not since *Prozac Nation* has a memoir expressed a more fitting amalgamation of the vile truth of having a mental illness and coming out victorious in spite of it as well as *because* of it.

In spite of the main subject matter being very grim and dark at times, *A Very Thin Line* beautifully juxtaposes Sharma's story with the feeling of optimism and believing in yourself for anyone who's ever felt stuck between a rock and a hard place due to a mental illness.

A quote Sharma states towards the end aptly describes the feeling you're left with: 'If you happen to be in a room full of intimidating looks... you can always count on your reflection to smile back. Always.'"

- Neel Trivedi, *writer at dailywisdomwords.com,*
mental health advocate

A Very Thin Line:
My Journey with Bipolar

Contents

No one knew in the seed he had found,
What secrets it held before the rain...
In time there grew a tree in the ground,
Now out of Chaos, the Order came.

~

Rx Mundi

Foreword

by Tianna G. Hansen

I'm a strong believer, like Rohan, that what you put out into the universe you will receive back and that there is always a glimmer of light despite any darkness you face. After I took part in the Inside Out: Prison Exchange Program as an outside student during my freshman year of college, I put out into the universe that I wanted to see one of the inside students doing well on the outside. Four years later, completely by chance, I turned up to an event as a photographer for the local community newspaper I was working at and took a photo of a group of speakers for NAMI Bucks (National Alliance of Mental Illness of Bucks County). It wasn't until one of the guys said my name and asked me if I went to Arcadia University that I slowly recognized Rohan from my Inside-Out class. He had changed a lot in those four years, and most importantly – he was on the outside! I couldn't quite believe the chance and luck that brought the two of us together again after all those years, and that's one reason this book is so special to release from my small press, focused on turning trauma into art.

Rohan was the first inmate I spoke to during the Inside-Out course. I walked in as a scared college student into the middle of maximum security, unsure of what to expect or who would greet me.

Our small room in the middle of jail was a makeshift classroom with chairs set in a circle. I chose a seat that felt most comfortable, beside a man who seemed slightly out of place and set apart from the other prisoners in the room. I introduced myself and he told me his name was Rohan. The moment our eyes met, there was an unspoken connection that passed between us. I learned he had been a medical student before he got locked up and that he lived with bipolar. I really couldn't believe he was inside jail, locked up for a mistake he made in the throes of an episode. I still find it hard to believe today.

Rohan's story is one that is unfortunately all too common but rarely spoken about: the fact that an untreated mental illness can lead to a crime and jail time. So much of life is defined by the little decisions we make. One of the first things I learned from Rohan when we met up again on the outside was to follow the breadcrumbs of your life — the stepping stones of excitement that lead you to something greater. Those breadcrumbs are what brought us back together and what bring you this book today.

As Rohan puts it, better than I ever could, chance is but a name for laws unseen.

This book explores how one decision can send you into a dark place, but no matter what, there is still the ability to find a light shining. No matter how dim or dismal your situation may seem, you can always make something positive out of it. Rohan's resilience is inspiring, to say the least. This book is not one for the faint of heart, but it will inspire and uplift you, no matter where you are in life. If you are someone who lives with mental illness, this book will prove to you that it gets better, no matter what you face. Sometimes you discover yourself in the most unlikely of places. For Rohan, that was inside jail. He is one of the most inspired and positive people I have ever met. I never expected, when I met him all those years ago inside jail, that he would become one of my best friends, but I am proud to call him that today and even prouder to call him my author and bring this book, his memoir of that time he spent in jail, into your hands.

Above all, live with an open heart, and read this with an open mind.

Preface

Some may think you need light in order to have a reflection. I am here to tell you about a different type of reflection — one that occurs even in the absence of light. This reflection is your outer world. The darkness occurs when you are in a place where there is little hope, a place where darkness is the norm. The Philadelphia Industrial Correctional Center (PICC) on State Road is one such place.

Out of the five county jails in Philadelphia, PICC is notorious for being the most violent. The inmates nicknamed it "Pokémon City," because it has the highest rate of stabbings, or people getting "poked." Not only is PICC packed with violent criminals, but the block which houses the mentally ill (where I was incarcerated for nearly two years) is a madhouse. There are fights nearly every day and corrupt correctional officers. It is a place where sanity and order are left at the door.

So, what do we do if we find ourselves in an environment where we cannot perceive light?

We create it.

I am here to tell you that there exists within each of us a Divine spark which will light even in the most heinous of places. I know this to be true and I hope by reading this book, this will become evident to you. It only takes a single candle to light a thousand, and its flame is never diminished in doing so. It spreads its light without limits, without bias, without hesitation. The brilliance of its light never fades as it spreads.

Floating down a river of despair gets you nowhere. There I was, holding on for dear life in rapids so tumultuous, I often look back and wonder how I survived. Was it all a dream? I carry scars that remind me it was not. It takes a strong mind and an even stronger will to survive, to navigate such treacherous waters. But the journey has been worth it since it has brought me to you — dear reader.

I would like to point out what led up to my incarceration: not getting the proper help I needed until it was too late. Keeping my emotions bottled and pretending everything was fine when in reality, my life was falling apart, splitting at the seams. My life went to an extreme which it may not have had to, and although I don't regret what happened (I am incredibly grateful) this does not mean what I went through is a path for everyone.

If you are reading this book while struggling with a mental illness, please get the help you need. There is always a way out, and life can become exceptionally better after you receive treatment. That is my promise to you.

*

I absolutely hate the term "Bipolar." I feel it fails to capture the severity this disorder can have on those it afflicts. To me, it suggests an occasional mood swing characteristic of what we all go through. Although it is a mood disorder, it's also much more than that. People who suffer from it can also experience wild delusions, as well as acute hallucinations and even psychosis.

Bipolar Disorder is a curious illness. Statistically, it affects 2.6% of adults in the United States, targeting both men and women equally[1]. Staggeringly, up to 1 in 5 people with this disorder can end up dying by suicide[2]. There have been celebrities who seem to have everything but have taken their lives despite their fame and success, which goes to show depression and mental illness does not discriminate based on socioeconomic status or tax bracket. Lives can be thrown into chaos by this condition, as my story demonstrates.

---

[1] These statistics according to Depression & Bipolar Support Alliance.

[2] Source: Goodwin FK, Jamison KR. Manic-Depressive Illness. New York: Oxford University Press; 1990

I have heard it said that if you could bottle and sell "mania," you'd become a millionaire. I have no doubt this is true. The world comes alive when you're in a manic state: the sun shines brighter, you may experience your television and radio speaking to you, you laugh hysterically to yourself, and you access ideas that you may have never been able to imagine otherwise. But there are downsides to this flight of unbound creativity. Delusions can become paranoia and take over, as they often have for me, sometimes culminating in indescribable depression, hopelessness, and loneliness I wouldn't wish on anybody.

This book is not so much a documentation of mental illness as it is a memoir of hope for those who may struggle (and those who don't). It's about overcoming the various challenges life may throw your way and choosing to be happy in spite of them. And therein lies the key word: choosing. Happiness is a choice – a lesson lost on me in my younger years but one I ended up learning anyways, albeit through a much rockier path. You don't have to go to jail or read the multitude of self-help books that I did in order to learn this lesson. You can put your foot down each morning when you wake up and make the conscious decision that, no matter what the day brings, you will be joyful because that is who you prefer to be. And even though I had to go to a Hell few will ever know in order to make this discovery, don't take it lightly when I say that I wouldn't trade this lesson for anything in the world.

Perhaps an equally important lesson was learned after I was released back into society. I knew it was true from my first-hand experiences in jail: your world is like a mirror, reflecting back your beliefs and definitions. Waiting for your life circumstances to improve before changing your state of being to what you prefer is like frowning in a mirror and waiting for your reflection to smile back[3]. I can tell you your reflection will always outlast you when it comes to who will smile first. Notice, however, that as soon as you smile, the mirror has no choice but to return the smile. If I had learned this early on, my life would have been much more enjoyable. But hindsight is 20/20, and it does no good to linger on prior experiences you wish were different.

---

[3] Bashar

Ever since I chose to define my illness as not an illness, but rather a gift, that's exactly how I've begun to experience it. Life is much better now, and I can honestly say I enjoy waking up and looking forward to what the day brings. But don't take my word for it. I'm a strong believer that you shouldn't take advice from anyone you don't want to end up as, for it will only make your life closer to theirs. So if you are in a position where you hate getting up to start your day, it can't hurt to redefine your circumstances in a way you prefer. Start telling a different story and watch the world around you change like magic.

*

Lastly, and I can't emphasize this enough, this memoir is not a jail survival guide. Time and time again, I saw inmates bigger than me getting jumped, and inmates smaller than me getting extorted. I was only able to make it through my time (and even thrive, as you will see in the following chapters) by what I believe was the grace of divine intervention. A dear friend of mine, Sandy, said that when she read this book, she saw God. I am not trying to convert any atheists, but my wish is to deter anybody from going down the same path who may think "he made it, so can I." If you are facing time in jail and you picked this book up hoping to gain some insight into jail life, my advice to you is this: be genuine in all situations, stay true to yourself, and perhaps most important of all, pray.

NOTE TO THE READER: I frequently use the word "bid" to refer to time in jail. I've also used the word "bit." The latter was the original slang term for a jail sentence. It morphed into the colloquialism "bid." That's what was used when I was in the "joint", an old expression for a "jail."

Stranger in the Mirror

"It is the way of weakened minds to see everything through a black cloud. The soul forms its own horizons; your soul is darkened, and consequently the sky of the future appears stormy and unpromising."

— Alexandre Dumas, *The Count of Monte Cristo*

Broken glass lay strewn everywhere around the small, dirty bathroom floor of my studio apartment. In my psychotic state, I shattered an empty beer bottle that was lying around; one of many. As I put one of the sharp fragments to my neck, I caught a look from the stranger in the mirror. He looked at me with eyes wide open. Despite not sleeping for almost a week and being physically exhausted, he had a maniacal look. As I peered deep into his irises, he stared back confidently as if to say, "Trust me."

With that, I sliced open the skin underneath my beard. I felt no pain as the result of swallowing the remainder of my Excedrin migraine pills (there were about eight left), and as the gash widened, I switched to using a pair of grooming scissors I had laying on the sink. As I cut away the skin at the edges of the laceration, blood began to stain the bathroom floor. I wondered why I didn't cut my jugular vein and end it all. This felt like more of a curiosity venture, opening my neck up and prodding around.

Everything in my subconscious mind came bursting out. I wrote the letters "D.M.T." in my blood on the   mirror. Dimethyltryptamine – the world's most powerful known hallucinogen. I experimented with it heavily during my senior year of college and as odd as it sounds, it felt like the only thing that kept me sane and allowed me to graduate. It had been my therapy; my release. Now my spirit yearned for it. But with no means to obtain it, my desperate plea for more went unanswered.

I took the sharp end of one of the glass fragments and began slicing my body. A feeling of relief poured over me with each cut. I turned around and looked at the blood around me, and as I did, my reflection sported the brand-new ink on my upper back. "Only God Can Judge Me," it read. The name of a song by the rapper Tupac now imprinted on my body forever. Why did I choose those words? I still didn't know for sure. I got it impulsively a few weeks prior, but in my delusional state, it felt right.

It was my fourth month into my first year of medical school and my mental illness had come out in full force. I had spent the previous month self-destructing – not going to class, failing my exams, drinking every night, losing the cash my parents had given me at the casino, and doing the only thing that kept me from diving completely off the deep end:; smoking marijuana. But now I had run out.

A drug dealer I met in the shady Germantown area of Philly had become my only real contact with the outside world. D was a rough looking, stocky, older African American man. After spending the night attempting to dissect my own neck, I called him up to ask if he could front me some more weed.

"You still owe me sixty dollars from last time," was his answer.

As he hung up, the first thought I had was how easy it would be to rob him. After all, the world wasn't real and I could do whatever I wanted, right? According to my delusions, other people were projections of my subconscious mind and had no volition of their own.

It was a crisp, Fall day as I walked out of my apartment. I popped the collar on my fleece to cover the gash in my neck as I waved to the security guard on my way out the door. A feeling of equanimity came over me and I was eerily calm on my way to the gun store.

Undiagnosed

"Someone I loved once gave me a box full of darkness.
It took me years to understand that this too, was a gift."

— *Mary Oliver*

It was the fall of 2011 and I was starting my first year at Drexel University College of Medicine, hoping to make my family proud. I didn't sleep the night before moving into my new apartment in East Falls, Philadelphia. Meeting the new students, I quickly noticed they all seemed to have it together.

I was barely hanging on by a thread.

Even orientation seemed overwhelming. My Bipolar Type 1 was undiagnosed at the time and what I later found out was "manic" behavior had become my normal lifestyle. Battling a severe addiction to Klonopin, I tried to get a year off in order to get my life together. The Dean refused two weeks before orientation, and I began scrambling to get all my paperwork and school supplies ready. It didn't take long for my apartment to look like a tornado had gone through it. The chaos of my outer living conditions mirrored the turmoil going through my mind. I pasted on a mask each day trying to fake my way like everything was normal. At night I didn't sleep. My thoughts raced like a movie set on fast forward that I couldn't turn off. During the day I would put my best effort into studying but I simply couldn't concentrate. Yet I still would go out for drinks with my classmates after exams as if I had something to celebrate. Life could not go on this way. Something had to give.

It was cloudy my first day sitting outside Dr. Amen's office. She was the school psychiatrist, and after weeks of failing exams and binge drinking, I knew I needed help. I explained to her what had been going on as she took notes.

"Would you say you drink more than other students?" she asked.

"I don't know. I guess," I replied. "All I know is I haven't been happy since I got here."

She ascribed this to depression and prescribed Citalopram. It is well-documented that antidepressants can induce manic episodes in people who are Bipolar, if not also taken in conjunction with a mood stabilizer. As the medication built up in my system over the coming days and weeks, my behavior grew more erratic. I was going to the gym at odd hours, and in order to burn off some of my manic energy, stayed there for exorbitant periods of time. I tried over the counter medications like Melatonin to help me sleep, but nothing seemed to work. Out of desperation, I began drinking almost every night in order to mitigate my racing thoughts. Finally, I resorted to what had always worked for me in college and I began smoking marijuana again.

At first, I started smoking socially with other medical students, but soon it became an obsession. I began hounding my classmates to see if I could score some for myself, but one by one they turned me down. Living right down the street from Germantown (a rough area of Philly), I realized I could score my own weed. It wasn't long until I found a drug dealer named D who would sell me what I needed.

The Day that Changed Everything

"I remember when I lost my mind. There was something so pleasant about that day."

— *Gnarls Barkley, 'Crazy'*

Ironically, the day I lost my freedom was one of the most liberating days of my life. It felt as if I were walking around in a dream; the sun shone brighter, food tasted better. It was almost like my Higher Self had come down in physical form and inhabited my body. I was extremely confident as I called a taxi service on my way to purchase the firearm that would be used in the armed robbery. Perhaps it was the effect of downing the remainder of my anti-anxiety medication – forty-two milligrams, or twenty-one times my prescribed dose.

It was the beginning of November, and I knew my parents wouldn't see the purchases I had made on their credit card until later in the month. I may as well have had a card with no spending limit, with how recklessly I was hemorrhaging money.

My neck began to hurt as the Excedrin migraine pills wore off. Dry blood crusted the inside collar of my black fleece.

"You can wait here," I told the cab driver, as we pulled up to the gun store. "This shouldn't take long."

The gun store was sparsely populated when I entered.

"What can I help you with?" said a pale, skinny man behind the counter.

"I'm not sure exactly. What kind of handguns do you carry?"

"Well we have a variety that might interest you," he replied.

As he pulled out a black Ruger from the glass display case, a different pistol caught my eye. It was silver and shiny, with a black handle.

"Can I see that?" I said, pointing to what would turn out to be my instrument of crime.

The .40 caliber Smith & Wesson felt cold and heavy in my palm. I didn't have a clear vision of what I was looking for when I went in the gun store, but this felt like it had been pulled right from my subconscious mind. The delusion I was in a dream only became more real.

"I'll take it."

As he swiped my parent's Visa, nothing felt amiss. While my peers were most likely in class, I was purchasing a gun so big, it could have probably taken out a large bear.

"Be careful with this one. Make sure you take it to a firing range first to get a feel for the recoil."

"Thanks," I said, leaving the store. Of course, I had no intention of doing that. I only had one thing on my mind – how good it would feel to inhale the sour diesel[4] I was about to score from D and finally get some sleep.

When the brain is severely deprived of sleep, it will go to any means to get the rest that it requires. I know this to be true, firsthand.

The whole scene felt like something out of a video game. Looking back, I find it shocking that it was that easy to buy a gun. The whole experience lasted about one hour, and in just a short cab ride, I was back at my apartment.

Now in the privacy of my room, I pulled the firearm out of the carrying case. I had never touched a gun in my life, but loading the ammunition came surprisingly easy. As I finished loading the clip like I was shown by the man at the gun store, I cocked back my new purchase and a single shell went flying. I caught it mid-air (like they do in the movies) and was satisfied things were going so smoothly.

---

[4] A particular strain of marijuana

The clean silver glistened in the sunlight that came through my studio apartment window. In my mind, I was in a world of no consequences. My inhibitions left me in my crazed state; they wanted no part in what was about to transpire.

I pulled out my phone and scrolled through my recent history. Several missed calls from my family and friends had accumulated over the past few days, and the rest simply said "D". In all my interactions with him, I still did not know what it stood for. Danger? Destruction? Dumb? It may as well have been all three.

My finger pressed on his shady moniker, and the phone began ringing.

"Yea?" he said. It was already late afternoon, and D sounded irritated.

"I got your money. I also need a dub[5]." Lying had become so casual to me, I almost believed it myself.

"Aight, come on through."

If he suspected anything, his voice didn't show it. Of course, what reason would he have to worry? After all, out of all his "clients," a medical student was the least likely to pull something.

Then again, it can be hard to predict the behavior of someone who is psychotic. Mental illness was the wildcard D did not count on.

I packed my newly acquired handgun into my backpack and slung it over my shoulder. What was I planning to do once I acquired the weed and finally got some sleep? Blow my brains out? I had no idea what I would do once the high wore off. As is often the case with addiction, I was only thinking about the short-term.

I walked down the same dubious street near notorious Germantown Avenue I had traveled dozens of times, but this day there was no shame. Not once did I second guess my decision. Why didn't I simply ask my parents for more cash? I'm sure my older brother would have given me some. Hell, there were a million ways I could have gotten money to pay D and supply me with the weed my brain desperately craved. In my manic state, however, there was only one solution.

---

[5] Slang for $20 worth of drugs

I stood out like a sore thumb in the area where D lived. With the area being predominantly African American, I was perhaps the only Indian for miles. As I came up to D's door, a group of young men hung out across the street at a local corner store. They eyed me while I pulled out my cell phone to call him.

"I'm outside," I said.

"Ok, be right there," was the reply.

D opened the door, and I walked in with no trepidation.

"I actually need another dub," I said, and D looked pleased. He closed the door to his small apartment while I remained in the walkway. With a door now shut in front of me and behind me, I slid the silver and black Smith & Wesson out of my backpack.

As he came through the door carrying two small sandwich bags of marijuana, I held the gun in front of me, drawn towards him.

Growing Up

I was an emotional kid. I would get teased in school because in the morning my eyes would tear up often for no perceivable reason. I never sought help, because in the very next class I would break out into fits of hysterical laughter, so much so that I went into denial that I even had a problem to begin with. My teachers probably didn't know whether to write me up or feel sorry for me. Often, my loud talking would disrupt the class and I played the role of nerdy troublemaker.

I fell into a mixed crowd, often paradoxical. In middle school, I was placed into all the advanced classes, but my gifted teacher was disappointed when I was suspended for throwing objects out of a school bus at passing cars on the way home from a field trip (we would have gotten away with it if Colin Bennett hadn't gotten overconfident and flung a Pepsi bottle at a passing car and broken its windshield). Still, I enjoyed the excitement of reckless behavior.

At age sixteen, I was arrested for vandalism with some friends. It was around the same time as the 2004 presidential election, and we went out the night before Halloween (mischief night) and stole various lawn signs in protest of George Bush. Driving around the rich area of town, we also shot pedestrians with a paintball gun, an act we were fortunate enough to get away with. I felt like a badass when the other kids at school found out and although my parents were embarrassed at the time since we had family visiting from out of town, we are now able to laugh about it.

My delusions began in middle school around the same time I started being bullied for being different. I often felt like I was special, and that my radio was communicating with me. When high school began, I was starting to feel like the world was all in my head. This led to some strange behavior such as obsessing over the news. I would scan the headlines daily in order to see how I was doing. A bomb going off in Iraq meant I had done something wrong, while conversely a positive story signified my mood was improving. How does one fit in society for so long with thoughts like these? I hid everything under a mask and did my best not to stand out. This resulted in often awkward and flat-out embarrassing situations, such as playing for our school football team where I mostly sat on the bench, or wearing my pants low trying to imitate my favorite rappers.

I cannot explain why I wanted to fit in and impress other people who I considered as only projections of my subconscious mind. You would think this would allow me to not care what people thought and sometimes this was true. I justified any awkward encounter after it happened by reminding myself of this fact, and it worked. My insecurities peeking out were okay at the end of the day because other people simply weren't real. Perhaps because part of me was still rooted in reality, I tried hard to make my parents proud.

A conversation my family had with me in high school was a profound turning point. They asked me what I wanted to be when I graduated college, and insisted I only had two options: either a doctor or a lawyer. I didn't want to be either. This made my depression worse as I felt like I didn't have a career to look forward to. But I talked myself into thinking I wanted to be a physician since other people were all a part of me anyways, and by healing them I would be healing myself. I didn't possess the courage at the time to tell them I wanted to join a monastery in Tibet and become a monk.

I ended up applying early decision to Carnegie Mellon University and after being accepted, I felt like I had made my family proud. Ironically, this is about the same time my migraines started getting worse. Perhaps my body was trying to signal this was not the path for me, but I ignored every repetitive signal, until I graduated with Honors. Getting started at Drexel University College of Medicine was much more challenging. Where I managed to work hard and keep it together for four years, medical school was a different beast. I was twenty-one during my first year of medical school, the age when mental illnesses often peak.

I came home one weekend to do my laundry, and I explained to my parents how I felt like I was two different people. I didn't know how to properly express the inner chaos I was feeling, and this was the only warning sign my parents received before I had my manic episode.

Rock Bottom

"And I know, knew for sure, with an absolute certainty, that this is rock bottom, this is what the worst possible thing feels like."

— Elizabeth Wurtzel, Prozac Nation

"Are you 5-0[6]?" D said in his raspy voice, shaking while he stared down the barrel of my .40 cal.

"Where's the ounce at?" I said, unphased. "Give me the rest of what you got!"

D led me up the stairs with my gun at his back and we passed by what appeared to be a little girl's room before entering his. He lifted his mattress where he and his wife slept, and there lay eight small sandwich bags filled with marijuana.

"Please, my wife's about to come home," D pleaded, his voice shaking.

"Throw them on the floor!" I shouted, and he picked them up one by one. After not sleeping for four days, I had become a real asshole. After pocketing the weed, he threw a wad of cash at my feet. I didn't care about the money but put it in my pocket as well. Suddenly, the sound of someone walking up the steps – D's wife. She reached the top and began to turn the

---

[6] Slang for "police"

corner when her eyes met the enormous gun pointed at her husband and she ran back down screaming. Not bothered in the least, I continued with the armed robbery.

I had put all eight small bags of marijuana in my pocket, each one a precious, tiny green treasure that would allow me to find sleep. What I didn't realize was just how serious the situation had become. Or what D was about to do.

We both heard shouting and loud banging coming from the downstairs door from which I had entered. It sounded like a mob of angry young men. Perhaps D's wife had told the group of men across the street what was happening, and they had come to his aid. D, maybe seeing concern on my face for the first time, was quick to answer.

"You can go out the back!" he suggested, as if reading my mind. Growing increasingly desperate, I followed his lead down the steps.

The hallway leading to his backdoor was extremely narrow, giving D the opportunity he was waiting for. He grabbed for the gun when my side was facing him, and we began to grapple for it. Being much smaller than him and given the fact that I had not slept in days, I still don't know how I was able to wrestle with him for what seemed like an eternity.

"I got the gun!" he shouted through the door.

Thinking quick, knowing that otherwise my time was up, I shouted back.

"Y'all come through that door, an' I'm gonna blow his fuckin' head off!"

My bluff worked and the door remained shut. Unsure of what was happening on the other side, they decided to not take the risk but instead shouted threats of what they were going to do to me.

"We're gonna fuck you up!"

I had more immediate concerns, as D had now managed to wrestle the gun so that the barrel was pointing at my right thigh. His finger squeezed on top of mine which lay on the trigger, but thankfully the safety was on. I remembered the man who sold me the gun had explained that in order to fire the gun, you needed to squeeze the tip. Feeling my manic strength giving out on me and knowing it could be only moments before his finger slid down and irreparable damage was done to my body, I let go and ran for the back door. My backpack caught in it and I slung it over my shoulder, releasing it to fall on the   ground behind me. My Drexel ID card was attached to it, but that thought only came to me later as I now heard police sirens out front.

I sprinted to the same main road I had so casually walked up only a little while earlier, but now it was getting dark and the street was filled with cars rushing home from work. Three gunshots rang through the air, causing me to stumble and lose one of my shoes. My front tooth hit the pavement, chipping it before I pulled myself up and ran straight into traffic; yet another memento I left at the scene of the crime. I was not sure who was doing the shooting, but I knew they would have to stop if they wanted to avoid any innocent bystanders who happened to be driving by.

A car swerved and almost hit me but kept on driving despite my pleas for them to stop. By the grace of God, the next car stopped and allowed me to get in, and I quickly shouted for him to drive away fast. He was a younger African American man, but at that moment he was an angel – who unknowingly happened to be playing the role of getaway driver.

"They're shooting," I said. "I need to get to the hospital." Quickly switching into the role of victim, the gash on my neck had reopened during the scuffle with D, and with blood coming out of it, I lied and said I had been shot in my neck. We sped to Temple Hospital, and I sneakily emptied my pockets of weed out the window. I knew what I had done was wrong in the eyes of the law, but when you are in a manic state, you aren't thinking about the people you are hurting, or any consequences for your actions. Still feeling no remorse for what I had done, and not intending on getting caught, we made our way to the hospital entrance, where the man who had driven me explained to some workers what he thought was the situation. From there, I was put onto a hospital stretcher, and wheeled into a vacant area which was closed off by some curtains.

Medical staff swarmed around me and examined the damage I had done to my neck.

"This doesn't look like a gunshot," said a nurse. They cut open my sweater in order to get a better look at the gash, and along with my shirt, my story also came undone as a number of other cuts were revealed.

"How did you get these?" one of the staff asked. I admitted I had done them myself, and they began seeing through all the lies. Hysterical, and even more sleep deprived and manic, I shouted at the top of my lungs.

"I'm off my meds! I'm off my meds!" I began laughing like a lunatic, and nothing mattered to me anymore. I received stitches for what I had done to my neck, but shortly after, detectives showed up to get my side of the story. I tried to play it off as if D were trying to rob me but was only incriminating myself further. More police showed up and I was handcuffed to the hospital bed. Still not seeing the severity of the situation, one of the officers turned to his partner and said, "So this is what rock bottom looks like." With that, I was placed in the back of a paddy wagon with other soon-to-be inmates.

At no point had any of the officers read me my rights, or even said I was under arrest. Maybe with the way I was behaving, they didn't think it mattered. They could have said anything. My word no longer had value. I felt like I was the lowest piece of shit on earth. The thought of what my family would say had no meaning to me. The intake process didn't even feel real. A Hispanic man asked what I had done to get locked up, and when I told him, he said armed robbery was worth up to fifteen years in prison. He may as well have said I had won the lottery. It didn't matter. Nothing mattered.

Fade to Black

"Sometimes we need to be knocked down in a place so dark that we have no choice but to trust our heart to illuminate the way."

— *Brittany Burgunder*

After I gave my fingerprints, my photo was taken for my mug shot. A man said I had to sign a piece of paper saying I understood the charges against me. When I asked where they were taking me, another inmate said, "the big boy jail." One of the guards told me I had one phone call I could make, so I pressed in my family's home number. After several rings, I hung up. What would I even say? I hadn't even processed what just happened, so how could I find the words to explain it? Still running on no sleep, my situation was growing desperate as the intake process dragged on.

When I explained what happened to my neck to an inquiring member of jail staff, I was placed in a separate cell by myself. Other inmates asked why I was put in a special cell, and the officer outside replied, "He's suicidal."

"If he's suicidal, put'm in here with us! We'll take care of him!" They laughed and barked threats from their holding cell. From there, they took me to the suicide wing of the Detention Center (DC), where I had to remove all my clothes and put on a green smock. The jail psychiatrist came and asked me some questions. I answered them truthfully, and she told me that I had Bipolar Disorder, which Dr. Amen had suspected herself, but never told me the antidepressants were what was causing me to become more manic. She explained it was an easy diagnosis, given that antidepressants are known to induce manic episodes in people with Type 1 BP.

The antipsychotic medication took a few days to kick in, but slowly, my delusions came crashing down one by one.

I did not have superpowers.

I was not special.

I had just attempted an armed robbery and was facing serious time in upstate prison.

As my bleak reality stood staring me in the face, panic began to set in. What had I done? Is this what the real world was like? Out of all the jail staff, the psychiatrist was the only one who seemed sympathetic to my situation.

"Here, you can call your family from my office phone. I already explained to them what happened. They're coming to bail you out."

No they're not, I thought. The jail staff are just trying to set me up. My delusions had gone but an intense fear took over the likes of which I cannot begin to describe. I was already in a terrifying situation, but my paranoia made it seem a million times worse. I felt like one of the inmates was going to stab me, or I would be raped. One of the inmates in the hospital wing had gold teeth, and I still remember him laughing at my plight. Another was mentally ill and thought he was Michael Jackson. I was convinced the only way out was suicide, but the staff took extra precautions in the hospital wing to make that next to impossible. I contemplated that I could steal one of the officers' tasers and shock myself, or perhaps unstring the thread from my orange jumpsuit and hang myself. Both seemed far-fetched, so I did the only thing my unstable mind could think of and attempted to rip the stitches out of my neck. It was incredibly painful, but when your mind is overtaken with that level of fear, you grasp at any futile attempt you can to end it all.

"Why are you crying now?" a correctional officer asked. "You wasn't cryin' when you did what you did!"

It felt like nobody understood or cared that I had a mental illness. I didn't fully understand. All I knew was this was the most terrifying situation I had ever been in, and I kept praying for death.

Anytime I made a serious attempt to hurt myself, the jail staff in the hospital wing would give me an injection. I would wake up dazed and praying it was all a dream, only to be reminded of the mess I had created. It turned out the judge had put what is known as a "detainer" on me, meaning I couldn't get bailed out until the court stipulations had been met. In this case, I needed a psych evaluation from the court psychiatrist. When I finally got in to see him, I lied about my delusions.

"Do you feel like you're special?"

"No."

"Do you think you have superpowers?"

"No."

I wasn't sure why I lied, but my paranoia had gone to a whole new level and I didn't trust anybody. I was sure they were sending me to upstate prison, where I was going to get stabbed. When the correctional officers told me I was getting bailed out, I didn't believe them. I thought they were setting me up, and when they placed the bail papers in front of me, I thought I would be signing away my freedom.

"I'm not signing shit," I told them. Finally, I resigned to my fate and signed the paperwork. To my surprise, they brought me to my dad. Even though I was shocked and overjoyed to be released, I still couldn't shake the suicidal ideations from my mind.

Eye of the Storm

"When someone makes a decision, he is really diving into a strong current that will carry him to places he had never dreamed of when he first made the decision."

— *Paulo Coelho*

After my parents paid my bail, I had a new appreciation for what it was like to be in medical school. When I finally got around to checking my Facebook, I saw it was filled with messages of classmates asking where I was. Some reached out asking if everything was okay. Little did they know how serious my situation was.

I had no idea what to tell my peers.

"Say you were sick, and you were getting help. Everything's fine, but now you'll be taking a year off and you'll be back next year. Just leave it at that," my brother said comfortingly.

I also received an email from the Dean at Drexel University College of Medicine (DUCOM), saying that the police had found my Drexel ID at the scene of the crime and called him. They explained everything regarding the armed robbery, and he stated in the email that I was not to set foot on campus except to meet him at his office.

"What were you thinking?" he exclaimed when I finally got the chance to meet him in person.

I didn't have an answer. Looking back, I realize it isn't really fair to ask someone who was in the midst of a psychotic break "what they were thinking." Psychosis, by definition, means losing touch with your external reality.

Four months later, I was expelled. All my years of studying and hard work completely gone because of a single night. Over twenty thousand applicants applied to Drexel College of Medicine the year I got in. Only 206 students had been admitted, giving it a 1% acceptance rate. This fact, which I had been so proud of, now meant nothing. Still trying to keep up the charade that everything was fine, I told people I was going to take an extra year off to do research in a lab. This only added to the weight of the already suffocating mask I had been wearing.

My family was instructed by the criminal defense attorney they had hired not to tell anyone what had happened. Keeping everything bottled up took a toll on my mental and emotional health. Tensions were high at home. It felt like my parents would argue about money every day, constantly reminding me they had spent upwards of twenty-thousand dollars in lawyer fees, in addition to the two grand spent bailing me out for that "stupid thing I had done" as my dad put it. Feeling like shit became my new norm. I had no self-esteem. My older brother was finishing his third year of medical school while I was living at home stealing Xanax from one of my family member's prescription bottle. I still remember them arguing on the phone with the pharmacy asking why they were short so many pills, as well as the look of sheer disappointment when I finally admitted it was because of me.

After a year and a half of fighting the case, I was ready to move on with my life. While out on bail I had managed to gain nearly forty pounds, get fired from two jobs, and isolate myself from my friends and family even more. I was filled with self-hate more than I could ever remember in my life. All I wanted to do was get high. I lied to all of my former medical school classmates. I lied to everybody, even my therapist.

The first deal the court offered me was three to five years in upstate prison.

I turned it down.

The lawyer my parents hired was able to get me placed into what is known as Mental Health Court, where they are more lenient towards your case given you have a mental health condition. This left me with two options. One, I could take the new deal they offered me (twenty-three months in county jail, followed by ten years of probation) or take it to trial. Oblivious to how the court system worked, I naively asked him if I lost at trial, could I still take the deal. His response to me was "you can't have your cake and eat it too."

I learned that the reason the courts offer plea bargains in the first place is to expedite the legal process, and to avoid going to trial, thus saving the city time and money. He warned me that I should not go to trial if I wasn't prepared to lose. Under no circumstance was I prepared to do five to ten years and given that twenty-three months was extremely lenient for an armed robbery, the decision to take the deal was a no-brainer for me. He also assured me I would be placed on the mental health block of jail and it was safer than the rest of the jail. Thinking the hospital wing I had been on was the mental health block, I agreed. What I didn't know, however, was that the block where I was about to serve my time was not the same hospital block I had been on. I thought I would be going to the same wing where I had my own cell, and things were relatively safe. I was unaware I was actually going to A block – or as it's known to the rest of the jail, "the fight block."

First Arriving at PICC

"The unknown is the only place you will ever actually discover your True Self."

— *Bashar*

There was a calmness at home in the weeks leading up to my sentencing. I took solace in reading a Hindu holy book by the name of the Bhagavad Gita. My dad read the papers. One story he showed me in particular remains in my memory to this day. Not because of the actual article, which I barely skimmed, but for the fact that the accompanying mug shot made the man look downright evil. I remember my dad made a comment that he looked like a demon. Little did I know I would soon be living in a cell with him.

The day I got sentenced left me with mixed feelings. Even though I knew I was embarking on what would be a difficult journey, I was relieved to end the waiting process. I felt like the criminal justice system had dragged out my case far too long, giving me monthly status hearings that ultimately didn't lead anywhere. On the day I signed my plea bargain and was taken into custody, my father said he was proud. He had seen me self-destruct for a year and a half while out on bail and was pleased I decided to finally move on with my life. Of course, this was coupled with the fact that he was losing his son. Growing up in India, he and my mom had no idea of the level of violence that went on in American jails. My mom later told me he cried that day.

As the prosecutor read back the police report in front of the courtroom, it brought flashbacks from what occurred that night. One line stood out among the rest.

"Police fired three shots…"

I knew I heard gunshots while running from the scene of the crime, but until that point, had no idea who was doing the shooting. I figured it was D, or one of the people on the corner of the block who had come running to his aid. The fact that it was the police made me realize the severity of my crime. It didn't matter to them that I was a medical student. They were responding to a call of an armed robbery in progress made by D's wife. To them, I was any other criminal. Up until that point, I didn't feel what I had done was so bad. Nobody had gotten hurt, after all.

As the officer took me out of the courtroom, my mind raced at what was ahead. My lawyer assured me that, because I was sentenced in Mental Health Court, I would be placed on a safer block. The irony was, the mental health block at PICC (A block) actually had the most 'full responses' called out of the entire jail, where guards would rush in to break up brawls that had gotten out of control (sometimes wearing riot gear, depending on the situation). Many of the inmates on A block were severely mentally ill, to the point where they couldn't function in society and kept returning to jail. What made this block so dangerous was many of them refused to take their medication and would snap for no apparent reason. Inmates fought over everything. I witnessed some who would argue with the air around them, lost in hallucinations. All it took was to accidentally bump into one of these inmates and it could lead to an all-out brawl.

When I went through intake, it was similar to when I had first gotten locked up; changing from cell to cell as the process dragged, interviews with jail staff including a multitude of nurses, as well as the safety check where we had to remove all our clothing, squat down and cough. This process took many hours and was demeaning to say the least. Being prodded along like cattle was not something my upbringing prepared me for. It put me in the mindset for how I would be treated by many of the staff in the coming months ahead.

"Here's your wristband. Your number is 1114732," one of the intake officers said, and with that, pointed me in the direction of inmates ready to shower before being placed on their respective blocks. The wristbands inmates are made to wear not only have what's known as our "PP number" on there, but also our mug shot. I had not seen mine in quite some time and found it hard to look at. I looked exhausted and disheveled, and the gash on my neck could be seen bleeding through my bandages after it had been stitched. It annoyed me knowing I would probably have to explain the full story of what happened every time someone looked at it. I took comfort in the other bracelet I was wearing, however; a red piece of twine known in Hinduism as a "kalawa" my mom had tied around my wrist for good luck. That didn't matter to the correctional officer watching us shower, and he made me tear it off. I wasn't as religious as my mom, but it felt violated having to throw it in the trash.

I would soon have bigger problems to worry about.

New Fish

"It is not the strongest of the species that survives, nor the most intelligent that survives. It is the one that is most adaptable to change."

— *Leon C. Megginson*

My first impression when I arrived on A block was absolute fear. When I first walked in, many of the inmates were watching TV in a large open area I later found was called the dayroom. Some turned their heads to stare, revealing scars and face tattoos like I had only seen in prison movies.

So much for trying to blend in.

An assortment of prisoners walked around, and as I was handed my sheets, a toothbrush, a yellow plastic cup and a red plastic spoon, I was told I would be moving into cell number 30. My cellmate was a husky older African American man by the name of Briggs, with a similar build to D. The cell was small, and my mind raced with worry as I pictured what would happen if Briggs and I were to get in a fight in such small quarters. After introducing myself and asking him what he was in jail for, Briggs explained he was in there for aggravated assault, and was on the mental health block because he was schizophrenic.

"So you hear voices?" I inquired.

"Yeah," he replied in a raspy, deep voice.

"What do they tell you?"

"Kill people."

In all my years at Carnegie Mellon, none of my roommates had ever said something like that. Even when my roommates and I argued, I never had to fear for my safety. This was a different story. I unpacked my paltry belongings and set up my bed. Briggs said I had to get the top bunk.

My first week on A block was an absolute nightmare. Until that point in my life, I could not recall a single real fight I had witnessed in person. Yet here, there appeared to be several each day. I still remember the first fight I witnessed in jail. A severely mentally ill inmate named Nasir was punched in the face by one of the laundry workers. Blood spattered the tiles as the correctional officers stood by and laughed. I later found out Nasir was HIV positive.

Why isn't anyone stopping this? I wondered. Shocked, I watched the jail guards egg on the fight.

"You gotta get me out of here!" I said, pleading to my parents over the phone as I realized the mistake I had made. It was as if all my fears and nightmares had congregated together and I was now living inside them. The only real experience I had of jail prior to being incarcerated was watching shows on TV. Safe in my home, I could even laugh at some of the inmates and what they were saying.

Here, there was nothing funny.

Life had caused me to live out one of my worst fears and I found myself face to face with the very same people I would usually only see on the evening news. I did everything I could to avoid eye contact, especially with the angrier inmates, but I found myself drawn to a man by the name of Emmett. The other inmates nicknamed him Jabba, after the Star Wars character "Jabba the Hut" for his tremendous size. He had lost a lot of weight but was still obese and stood towering over many of the other inmates. What drew me to him was his sense of humor. We started talking and I found out he was also from Bucks County, the town of Bensalem, which wasn't too far from where I lived. He explained that he was locked up for causing a disturbance on SEPTA, the public transit system. Jabba said he missed his stop, and the SEPTA workers told him he had to make his way off the train.

That's really unfair, I thought, believing every word.

This resulted in an argument where he pulled out a knife. After getting off at the next stop, police were there and fired shots at him while he said he ducked behind a car. I was still naive at this early stage as to how jail is full of liars and people who embellish their stories. Although it is possible that he was telling the truth, given what I know now, my money would be on him being full of shit. Still, something about his story seemed vaguely familiar, but I just couldn't put my finger on it.

I had seen him get into altercations in my first few weeks and he seemed to intimidate many of the smaller souls on A block, so I was happy to be in his good graces. What I didn't know at the time is that many inmates will act nice in order to get something from you or manipulate you. I was just a new fish who had been thrown into a shark tank, and eager to make friends out of fear of other inmates stabbing or, even worse, raping me. He suggested I move in with him, and I naively thought it was a good idea at the time. I quickly found out it was a mistake.

Never Let Fear Decide Your Fate

"If you behave like a victim, you become a victim."

— *Anonymous*

We had a blast that first night in Jabba's cell. I hadn't laughed so hard in quite a while, and we talked for hours, jumping from topic to topic. He gave me some insights into jail life, including how inmates put raspberry juice packets in milk, which makes it taste almost like strawberry milk. His cell was in what is known on A Block as "the projects." It was the grimy area in the back hallway where inmates would often go to fight without getting caught, or smoke teabags (more on that later). Lots of illicit activity went on in that dark, dirty hallway, and CO's would usually only visit when they were making their rounds, going cell to cell to check on inmates. I learned of more illegal activity that would go on there later in my sentence; stuff even a convict like Emmett didn't know about.

I said to him how this had to be synchronicity, a word I had picked up from one of the strange books on the paranormal I had read when I was a kid.

"How do you spell that?" asked Jabba, pulling out a pen and paper.

After I told him, we went back to cracking jokes and laughing. I happened to glance up from the bottom bunk and my eyes caught something which had been written on the cold, metal above me. There were very vulgar thoughts written out, each one starting with the name

"Trevis." I decided not to bring it up to Jabba, and put it in the back of my mind, hoping to never run into whoever this Trevis was. He was obviously very sick and needed help, but this would be the first harbinger of things to come. The next sign that this was a wrong move for me was when Jabba showed me his wristband, which had his mug shot on it. My jaw dropped as I instantly recognized the picture as the one from the newspaper my dad had showed me only weeks prior – the one my father thought was a demon. I could not believe fate had put me in the same cell as the man in that photograph. I mentioned to Jabba that I had seen his picture in the paper and wondered if my mug shot had been showcased in the media as well. I prayed that it hadn't.

Shortly after that night, things started to turn dark. Certain details about Jabba's stories seemed to not add up, and it felt like he was trying to turn me against everyone in the jail.

"You see those vents? They spray gas through them in order to get you while you sleep. It makes you impotent so you can't have kids, it's all part of their plan to get rid of black people."

"That seems a little far-fetched," I replied. Jabba got furious, and I was starting to see why he was on the mental health block. His diagnosis was Bipolar Type 1, like me, but his delusions were often paranoid, and his mood became unstable in a way I should have been able to see coming.

One day, a monstrous cockroach found its way into our cell. Jabba stomped it out and explained to me that a correctional officer by the name of Grayson (who I had begun to like) had placed it there on purpose. Now starting to see through his web of lies, my time in jail started to become an everyday struggle. He talked incessantly, and I found it hard to read the books my mom had sent me and be polite at the same time. I wanted to move out but knew it would be risky as Jabba would take it personally and could turn violent. I needed an excuse, and he gave me the perfect one.

Nearly a month into my sentence, I hadn't expected what was to come next. Jabba had taught me how to fill out commissary sheets, and with the money my parents put on my books, I was able to get the basics: underwear, shower shoes, soap, shampoo, as well as some snacks which I shared with Jabba. But his greed was no match for the politeness my parents had instilled in me growing up, and I quickly realized I was being taken advantage of. He convinced me to get a radio off of commissary, and I thought music would make the time go faster. When it finally came in, I immediately put in new batteries and headphones. "Get Lucky" by Daft Punk featuring Pharell was playing, and it instantly gave me a taste of being free again.

"Can I listen?" came Jabba's booming voice, after a few carefree hours went by. I figured it couldn't hurt, given it was only a radio. He was my "cellie," after all, and I was fully reliant on him for protection from the other inmates at this point in my sentence. The next thing I knew he was singing along at the top of his lungs. When I asked if he could keep it down so I could read, he refused.

This continued on for several days. Life had become a nightmare. My only solace was getting visits from my mom every Tuesday and Thursday, as well as the books she would mail to me. She sent me the Bhagavad Gita so I could finish reading where I had left off while out on bail, as well as *A Brief History Of Time* by Stephen Hawking. My favorite subject in college had always been physics, and now with seemingly all the time in the world, I figured I could use some of it to get to know the Universe a little better. I was fascinated by it and quickly finished the book amidst the jail fights as well as Jabba's unbearable gas. It was an interesting juxtaposition to say the least.

Then one day, Jabba stopped taking his medication, and I noticed he was more irritable than usual, and more paranoid. Listening to the radio until I fell asleep had become my usual routine, but this night I was awoken by Jabba asking to borrow it. It must have been around one in the morning, and I fell back asleep after saying I was still using it. I was awakened several hours later by him, again, asking to borrow the radio. Knowing he would most likely sing at the top of his lungs if I gave him the radio, and I wouldn't be able to sleep, I refused for a second time. That's when Jabba had enough.

"Give me your fuckin' radio before I take that pen an' stab you in your fuckin' throat!" he shouted.

I was shocked and terrified of losing my life at something so trivial. I handed him my radio. It must have been close to 4 AM by this point, and perhaps the most terrifying part of this ordeal was no one would have even been able to hear me scream from all the way in the back hallway. The CO on duty had already done his rounds and may as well have been miles away at that point.

It was just me.

And Jabba.

Trapped in a small, nine by thirteen[7] foot cell.

He barked threats at me for what seemed like an eternity. As the hours went by, my fear turned to anger, and morning couldn't come soon enough. When the CO finally came around to give us our breakfast trays, it was around eight in the morning. Still recovering from the shock of what had just happened, in combination with the terrible food they were serving, I couldn't recall ever being less hungry in my life. I knew I needed to tell the CO what had transpired, but with Jabba around, I still didn't feel safe.

To my surprise, after he ate his breakfast, Jabba handed me back my radio and said he was sorry. I was quiet the rest of that morning, but as soon as it was time to line up for medication, I saw my chance. I exited 39 cell pretending we were still cool, and when I went to get in line for medication, asked Miguel (an inmate I had become friends with) if I could move in with him. After he said it was cool, I explained to the officer on duty that I wanted to switch cells but did not tell him the reason out of fear of being a "snitch." Officer Omari agreed, and I marched straight to 39 cell to pack up my things and get ready for the big move.

Jabba happened to walk in the cell before I finished gathering my belongings and asked what I was doing. I explained to him that I was moving in with Miguel because him trying to steal my radio "wasn't cool." That's when he became furious again.

"Aight, you can leave, but you're leaving that radio in here with me!" he shouted.

"I'm not leavin' my fuckin' radio, now get outta my way," I demanded. My newfound "courage" only came from the fact that our cell was now unlocked, and CO's were around.

"Okay, then you're gonna fight me for it!" he threatened, putting his hands up.

"I'm not gonna fight you for it, it's mine!"

With that he shoved me and swung his giant fist towards my face. It grazed my upper lip, taking skin with it.

---

[7] Could not confirm this was the dimensions, but this is what was commonly repeated

"That's enough!" shouted Officer Omari, who heard our argument and came bursting into our cell. "Jabba, step out! I said MOVE IT!"

His Caribbean accent sounded like music to my ears and with that, Officer Omari became my new favorite CO. I packed up the rest of my belongings (including my radio) and took it to Miguel's cell. I still didn't know how I was going to survive my time on A block. A few days later, rumors went around that a banger[8] was found in one of the bottom tier cells during a shakedown, and with Jabba out to get me, things were only getting more and more dangerous. That's when Miguel had a suggestion for me.

"You can just say you're suicidal to the nurse," he explained one day, while I was expressing my fears. Perhaps he was sick of my "bitching," but the idea still intrigued me.

"They'll move you to DC, where you'll have your own cell. You can't stay there long, but many inmates do it just to get off the block. I've done it myself."

Morning couldn't come soon enough. My plan was to stay in the hospital wing as long as I could and pray that when they put me back on the block, things would have cooled down or my family would have found a way to get me out somehow. I told the nurse while getting my morning medication that I was suicidal, and after filling out some paperwork, I was put in handcuffs and escorted to the receiving room.

I waited patiently for hours in a holding cell, and even though I knew it was a cowardly move, I felt safe. That is, until an inmate who was working there started laughing when he heard I was "suicidal," and started threatening me through the glass window.

"You better not come back to A block, 'cuz I know people there an' Ima make sure yo' ass gets whats comin' to ya," he said, as he made a stabbing motion with his hands.

I was terrified. I thought this was a safe way out, but it seemed like every time I acted out of fear, I only made the situation worse. Now, not only would I have to deal with Jabba when I came back to A block, but I thought any number of inmates could stab me.

---

[8] A makeshift sharp instrument, also known as a "shank"

Spider in the Storm

"If you have never reached rock bottom, you have never attended the school of greatness."

— *Matshona Dhliwayo*

Spending time in what is known as the "suicide wing" (back in the jail next door known as DC) was an altogether different experience. They only opened the door for five minutes every morning to converse with the psychiatrist, to deliver food three times a day, and once in the evening for medication. What kept me going was the fear of what awaited me when I returned to PICC. Would the inmate still be there in the receiving room? Did he really know people on my block? Was there a way for him to come on to A block? I paced around my bed feverishly. No soap was provided in these "suicide cells," and all clothes had to be removed. We were only given a green smock to cover our bodies, and it grew very cold at times. I couldn't speak to my mom over the phone as long as I remained in the suicide cell, and my mind raced with anxious thoughts. What if she had a heart attack? What if there was a car accident? Here, I had no cellie, and with my newfound privacy, I cried for the first time since I arrived.

Then one night during my stay there, a heavy rainstorm hit our area. The rain came pattering down against my small window, heavier than I could recall in quite some time. Outside I saw a spider's web, with a giant spider braving the rain. The wind tossed and turned the web furiously, but still the spider continued to hold on.

True, I was in a tough situation, I thought. But if I can just hang on like that spider, maybe I, too, can weather the storm.

Finally, I reached my wit's end. I realized there was only a certain amount of fear I could tolerate before something in me changed. If that inmate was going to stab me, then there was nothing I could do about it, but I wouldn't continue to stay in that cell a day longer and torture myself with fear. With that realization, I started working out to ease my anxiety by doing tricep dips, using the bed for support, as well as doing incline pushups. The next morning, I told the doctor I was no longer suicidal, and I signed some paperwork to get me off that dreadful block and into a nice, hot shower.

Seeking Magnanimity

"If you aspire to achieve great things in life you need magnanimity."

— *Abdul Kalam*

While out on bail, and especially during the first month of my sentence, I held a lot of hatred in my heart. Hatred toward society, toward the criminal justice system, even toward my former peers. Why did they get to remain free? Why was I the only one who had to serve time? I felt like my only real crime was smoking weed, which many of the other med students were also doing. I even reached out for help to the school psychiatrist, and that only ended up exacerbating my problems. It's well established in medicine that when a patient goes without sleep for long enough, their brain will go to any lengths to get it. I didn't choose to be born with a mental illness; did that really give society the right to take away my freedom for something I did while in a psychotic state? After all, nobody got hurt (aside from the damage I had done to my own body). It took some time for me to acknowledge that the hatred I felt was merely a reflection of the hatred I already had towards myself.

You hear it all the time: "life's not fair." People are born into certain situations, and it's just the luck of the draw, right? When I first began my sentence, I felt like I was one of those who just happened to be dealt a shitty hand in life. Now a convicted felon, I knew the odds would be even greater against me when I was back on the outside – if I even made it through my time. When my parents got a consultation with an educational lawyer to fight my expulsion from medical school, something he said really stuck with me:

"Son, you plead guilty to those charges and your life is over. The best you can hope to be when you come out of jail is a janitor."

But my brother reminded me of something important when I repeated back what the educational lawyer had said.

"You still have this," he said, pointing at my head. "Not everyone is fortunate to have your intelligence, and as long as you have that, you have everything."

My brother's words played a role in my decision to plead guilty. That, and the fear of what would happen if I lost at trial.

It didn't help that one of the first books in jail I asked my family to mail to me was *The Count of Monte Cristo* by Alexandre Dumas. It's widely considered to be a classic, a tale of revenge set in the 19th century. The main character, Edmond Dantes, is falsely imprisoned by a group of men who are jealous of him. He is sentenced to life in *chateau d'if*, a French prison with absolutely horrid conditions. Fourteen years into his sentence, he manages to escape and finds a treasure buried on the Isle of Monte Cristo. Now with his freedom and vast wealth, he uses his power to exact revenge on those who wronged him, one by one. The story had a lasting impact on me during my twenty-three months, and still does to this day.

There were so many people and establishments I felt like getting revenge against, but the main theme of the story resonated with me. Dr. Amen, the one who prescribed the anti-depressants in the first place, wouldn't return my phone calls or emails while I was out on bail and fighting for my life. But the ending to the book displays a powerful message: Edmond Dantes finds no peace once he successfully takes down each of the men who set him up. Not wanting to end up in the same predicament, I knew forgiveness was going to be key if I ever wanted to make peace with what happened.

Magnanimity is defined as the state of being able to forgive, and I spent many nights in jail pondering if I would ever find it. Perhaps with enough time and maturity, I could muster up forgiveness towards society, and the people who I felt wronged me. But could I ever reach that state of being magnanimous toward myself?

Meeting Trevis

Fortunately, the jail staff housed me in the hospital wing for two weeks before they decided that I was okay to go back to A block. The female nurse who was taking my vital signs noted that I had lost ten pounds during the week I spent in the suicide cell. I knew this was due to the intense fear and anxiety that plagued me, as well as the furious pacing I did in my cell each day. The hospital wing, though, was like a nice vacation from all the madness I experienced my first two months in; people getting beaten, deranged lunatics shouting and banging on their cells all night, as well as the awful smell. The wing they put me on was actually the same wing I had been on when I first got locked up. Here, you had a cell to yourself. There was even a TV in the common area, along with apple juice. It was relatively drama-free, and I made friends with one of the inmates there named Farhan. He also came from A block and was placed there because he was schizophrenic.

I rarely loaned my books out, but Farhan and I developed a trust over the course of a few days, and I thought he would enjoy a spiritual one my parents had sent me called *Siddhartha*. We had several intellectual conversations, but I was still shocked to learn he had studied economics at UPenn when he was younger before his first psychotic episode ended up getting him incarcerated. Now in his thirties, jail had become a revolving door for him. He explained to me that he kept hearing voices and they told him to do terrible things, like set things on fire. When the voices first started, he was a student at UPenn and one day, they instructed him to

53

start walking. He ended up walking all the way from campus to New Jersey, where the voices ordered him to enter someone's home and take all of his clothes off. Unfortunately, there happened to be a family living there at the time. With a little girl. Now a registered sex offender, he was expelled from college and had been in and out of jail ever since.

I also loaned him *The Grand Design* by Stephen Hawking (one of my personal favorites), but he said he had trouble understanding some of the concepts. Then one day he told me about a particular voice in his head. "His name is Trevis, and he tells me to hurt people. He's the worst."

After inquiring if he ever lived in 39 cell, he replied that he had. It then became clear to me that the vulgar writing above my bed in the cell with Jabba was from Farhan. I was shocked, since he was so smart and had been so kind to me, I did not expect there to be a darker side to him. I felt bad for people like Farhan who heard voices and became even more grateful my mental illness was not as severe. Even after all I had done in my psychotic state, I could still function in society, which is something many of the inmates on A block could not claim.

An Angel Named Eli

I now had a new mindset from my time in DC. I was determined to make the best of my twenty-three-month sentence, and not just lay in bed all day in my cell out of fear. I started spending more time out in the dayroom and socializing with other inmates. I was still afraid, but I wasn't going to let that stop me. It seemed like the Universe rewarded my courage right away.

When I came back to A block, I was asked which cell I would like to move into. Q (Miguel's old cellie) had returned to jail and had moved back in with Miguel, but the CO on duty said 30 Cell had no one living in it at the time. Having a cell to myself was like a dream come true, and I eagerly moved my belongings into what would be my new home for the coming months.

Miguel made sure I was okay when I got back to the block, and for all he had done for me, I decided to give him my radio as a token of appreciation. I figured it had caused me enough trouble and I knew how much it would mean to him, since he loved listening to the rap stations. He was grateful, to come telling me to come to him if I needed anything. The CO had not given me a red spoon this time, and he happily got one for me. His cellmate Q came up to my cell and slid it under the door, and I got to know him a little as well.

Only a day had gone by when the CO informed me that I would be getting a new cellie. He was a skinny, older African American man by the name of Eli, and we took a liking to each other immediately. Eli and I cracked jokes for hours on end, and my sides hurt on more than one occasion from his brilliant sense of humor. His life situation was no laughing matter, as Eli explained to me that he smoked crack on the outside and was locked up for getting high while on probation. No matter how hard he tried, he just couldn't seem to quit his addiction. He told me about the first time he was introduced to crack. Eli was a janitor at a hospital and was doing fairly well for himself, when one day, he saw a woman sitting on the doorstep to his apartment complex. He inquired if she was okay or needed anything, and after talking briefly, she came up to his apartment. She then pulled out a vile of crack and offered to sleep with him if he would smoke it with her. Not knowing just how addictive it was, Eli said it was the biggest mistake of his life.

Within only a matter of months he cleaned out his entire bank account (thousands of dollars, he claimed) to spend on crack. He was fired from his job, and like many other addicts before him, ended up stealing to feed his incessant addiction. It was not long until he was arrested for burglary, doing several years in Graterford – the most violent prison in all of Pennsylvania. I had heard horror stories about it from my time in jail, and Eli told me his tale of how he managed to survive. I was impressed with his mental toughness and inspired by his story of hardship. I hadn't been through even half of what he experienced in his life. Listening to his stories filled me with a sense of overwhelming gratitude.

"Only God can judge me?" Eli asked one day, looking at my upper back. I continued my vigorous workout regimen from when I was in DC (without a shirt, of course) and almost forgot I even had it.

"Yeah, just something I got when I was manic." I laughed.

"Well that's a true statement," he replied.

"Yeah, I guess you're right." I felt embarrassed when I initially got it, as some of the other med students questioned why I chose to get that phrase tattooed on me, and some even laughed at me. But in jail, it felt like inmates understood the meaning of those words, with some even coming up to me saying they were going to get it as well.

The time started to go by quickly while I was cellmates with Eli, and I was motivated to start a new gratitude regimen. Each night, despite anything that happened during the day, I thanked God for anything that came to mind. I thanked God for bringing Eli into my life, for the health of my family, for the multitude of books I was blessed with, as well as for allowing me to keep all my teeth (I'd seen inmates get their teeth knocked out and this had a profound effect on me). I told myself, as long as I had all my teeth each night, I was thankful.

A self-help tip which I implemented around this time also helped my life take off to a whole new level. It was the practice of defining whatever came up as "good." I learned that no situation has any built-in meaning to it; circumstances are like a neutral set of props. It is you who gives meaning to any situation, and a simple story I read in one of the self-help books my mom sent me helped illustrate this point:

There once was a king and he had a friend who, no matter what happened, always said, "This is good." One day, the king went hunting with his friend, but the rifle misfired and blew the king's thumb off. The friend said, "This is good," and the king, furious, decided to lock his friend in jail.

A year went by and the king went out hunting again, but this time, he was alone. He ended up getting captured by cannibals who tied him up. They were ready to eat him when all of a sudden, they noticed his thumb was missing. The cannibals happened to be very superstitious, and didn't eat anyone who was not whole, so they untied the king and set him free.

Overjoyed, the king goes to his friend in jail to tell him what happened and set him free. "You were right, losing my thumb was good!" said the king to his friend. "I'm so sorry I imprisoned you."

"That was good also," replied the friend.

"How could that be good? You were in jail for a year!"

"Because if I was not in jail, I would have been on that hunting trip with you, and the cannibals would have eaten me!"

This story helped me to see that no matter what came up during the course of the day, it was good. And by defining it as such, sooner or later, I would see that it was. Eli loved that story, so much so that when he was called into the head office by one of the CO's, unsure of why, he turned to me and said, "This is good!" Sure enough, they were processing his discharge paperwork so he could get released. I knew I was going to miss Eli, but I was also happy he was getting out. I felt confident that with this new self-help tip, coupled with my nightly gratitude, I had all the tools necessary to get me through my time.

A Friendly Face

During my time with Eli, a CO asked me if I wanted to start taking classes. At the time, my lawyer instructed me to get involved in as many positive activities as I could, as there was a chance the judge may let me out early for good behavior. The first course I started taking was one that taught inmates the power of breathing through meditation. I found it useful, and it helped ease my fear of getting off the block. The second was known as the "Inside-Out" program, where college students would visit the jail and interact with inmates. When I first signed up for the program, I didn't expect I would be forging a strong bond with one of the college students; one that would re-ignite years after I was released.

My first thought about Tianna when she walked in was how innocent she looked. Just your typical white, privileged college girl with no idea about how dark life could get. Perhaps being in jail for four months made me jaded, and it would be years later when our paths crossed again that I was able to see how wrong I was, and that stereotypes can work both ways.

I was excited to be back in a classroom setting (or as close to one as there was in jail), and surprised a real professor from Arcadia University would be coming in. Correctional Officer Grayson recommended the class to me as soon as he heard they were looking for inmates to fill the open seats in the class, and even though I was nervous about leaving A block once a week, I thought it would look good for my judge to see I was making an attempt to better myself in jail. I was nervous about our first day, even more so when I met the other inmates. Most of them came from D block

58

(the worker's block) and therefore already knew each other, and it was pretty obvious I was the odd one out. Before the college students came in, they asked me what crime I had committed.

"Armed robbery," my voice choked. "But it's not what you think," I said as I took in the puzzled look on their faces.

They all seemed surprised, a few even laughed. After making an attempt to explain the whole situation about my mental illness being misdiagnosed and being prescribed the wrong medication (even adding that I was in medical school when I had my psychotic episode) none of them seemed to understand. Now almost five months into my sentence, I was pretty used to the ignorant reactions of others. This only seemed to isolate me more from them, and I was eager to put the whole conversation behind me. Why couldn't I just keep my mouth shut? Maybe it was my desperate attempt to prove it wasn't my fault and that I hadn't just "fucked up," like I'm sure the rest of them had been perceived of doing. My endeavor fell on deaf ears.

"So, you were a doctor?" one of the bigger inmates, Rashid asked.

"No, I was still a student."

"And what were you robbing for? I know Indians got money."

"Weed," I stuttered. "I couldn't sleep and..."

The inmate who sat closest to me, Walid, told me I didn't have to explain and they were just messing with me.

Great, I thought.

I was already used to not making "smooth" first impressions, but that hadn't mattered during my four years at Carnegie Mellon, where I wasn't the only nerd. Here I was alone, and confidence didn't seem to be a problem for the other inmates in the class like it was for me.

As the college students came into our "classroom," I was surprised and a little disappointed to see there were only four of them. This meant I would only be more visible to the professor, as I couldn't simply hide in the back like I had planned. Overall, it didn't matter, since I was sure all the inmates would automatically get A's just for participating. But it wasn't the grades I was concerned about. How would the other students perceive me? Would they simply think I was "stupid" for getting locked up? Like I was a drug addict who had made a bad decision? That my life was just a lesson to be learned from? I felt I had to prove my "innocence," but how?

One of the ice breakers we played was a game called "two truths, and a lie." Like the name suggests, we each had to write down two facts about ourselves and come up with a lie. The object was to guess which of the three statements was the lie about the other people in the class.

Perfect, I thought. I'll slip in the fact that I was a medical student who just happened to be mentally ill, and then they'll see me as one of them.

After we had partnered up (two inmates for every college student), I went last. My three statements were as follows:

1. I was in medical school
2. I'm diagnosed as Bipolar Type 1
3. I'm originally from California

Emily, the college student I was partnered with, knew the lie right away (as you can probably guess by now, I'm not from California).

But the class seemed no different. No fanfare, no comments; no one seemed to care. After the students left that day, I felt disappointed. Why was I so desperate to tell my story? Who was I trying to convince that this all wasn't my fault?

It took me a long time to figure out that I was really trying to convince myself.

Don't Judge a Book by Its Cover

Coming out of my first "Inside-Out" class, I walked through the hallways with the other inmates on our way back to our respective blocks. I kept to myself and hung towards the back of the group. Suddenly, an officer appeared and stopped us.

"Where are your passes?" he inquired.

"We never got none," Walid replied.

Infuriated, the officer radioed for his superior to come. Shortly after, a lieutenant (or "white shirt" as they are known in jail) appeared to see what all the commotion was about. After learning none of us had any hall passes, a shouting match began to ensue between the officers and the inmates of the class. I wasn't sure what was going to happen and kept quiet, even though I felt like I didn't do anything wrong. To me, this was just another example of officers abusing their power, since obviously we were coming from a class and none of us were doing anything we weren't supposed to. I felt like we should just be allowed back to our blocks.

Finally, a sergeant came and stepped in. Once he understood what the issue was, he said we were free to go back to our blocks. Relieved, I began walking towards my block, this time in front of the other inmates.

All of a sudden, I heard a voice behind me say, "you know that was for you, right?"

It was Walid. Confused, I turned around to see what he was talking about. All eight other inmates pulled out their hall passes.

"We all had one. We just knew you didn't," he continued.

I'm still not sure how they knew I didn't have one, but I was stunned by their act of kindness. The correctional officers on my block hadn't given me a hall pass for some reason, and if I had been the only inmate without one, it was much more likely I would have gotten a write-up or had other issues getting back to my block. But there certainly was strength in numbers, and I was overwhelmed by the trouble the other inmates had gone through on my behalf. Perhaps they may have thought I was Muslim like them. In jail, Muslims look out for one another. Whatever the reason, it certainly felt like someone or something had my back. I was still learning how to acclimate to my surroundings, but that day taught me to never judge a book by its cover.

Necessity: The Mother of All Invention

Kindness wasn't the only part of the inmates which surprised me. I was now half a year into my twenty-three-month sentence, and I was really starting to pick up on the ins and outs of jail. One thing which never failed to impress me from the moment I got to A block was the extreme creativity which inmates showed in solving their problems. I witnessed the sheer brilliance of some of the prisoners on my block while playing chess, but what happened when the correctional officers weren't around was even more astounding.

I began to appreciate their ingenuity early in my sentence when I moved into 40 cell with Miguel. Q had just moved out so he had an open bed, and Miguel was one of the few inmates I connected with during my first month. He wasn't too much older than me, roughly in his early thirties, and we connected through our mutual love of rap music. He was also one of the inmates who looked out for me when Jabba tried to steal my radio, making him my top choice in terms of who I wanted to live with after I "escaped from the projects." We were making standard cellmate conversation; arguing which rappers were top five of all time (Big L, Nas, Andre 3000, Method Man, and Black Thought, of course) when he paused.

"Yo, you wanna get high tonight?"

Startled, I asked him how.

"Q left me some tea bags before he left."

"Tea bags?" I asked, confused.

63

"Yea, you can order them on commissary. You cut the bag and pour the powder into the tissue that the toilet paper comes wrapped in. Then you roll it up and smoke it."

"Uhhh…" I stumbled.

"It's not as strong as weed, but it'll still get you buzzed."

Curious, I asked how he was going to manage to light it.

"That's easy. I got two batteries. You put one facing up and one facing down on a metal surface. I use the sink. Then you get the twine from one of the bread bags from one of the block workers. Don't worry, our block rep, 8 Ball, already hooked me up."

Intrigued, I asked him to go on.

"You strip the plastic off the twine using some nail clippers, which you also get off commissary, so it's just down to the metal part. Cut it in half. After that, you touch each end of the twine to each of the two batteries, and when you put the two tips together, it starts to get really hot."

He showed me burn marks on his two forefingers.

"You can't hold on to it for too long, but you put the joint in your mouth and inhale as the metal starts to get red, and then it's lit!"

I looked at him in awe. It was one of the most ingenious things I had ever heard: to use metal twine from a bread bag to complete an electrical circuit between opposite poles of a pair of batteries. My mind was blown. They never taught that in college Physics.

"Chill bro, I'll show you how it's done. We're gettin' blazed tonight." He laughed. The extreme creativity of inmates was one of the higher points of my sentence; however, it was only a short time later that I was given a very dark reminder of where I was.

A Senseless Tragedy

Roughly six months passed before I got word that there was another Indian inmate in the jail. He was on K block, the other mental health block. Diagnosed with schizophrenia, he was arrested for a very petty crime: stealing a pack of gum from his family's convenience store. His bail was set at only five hundred dollars.

One day the jail went into lockdown, as it often did when a major fight broke out or there was another stabbing. The next day, a correctional officer named Jackson told me the real reason for the lockdown.

"You know that Indian kid hung himself, right?"

What a tragedy, I thought. Rather than pay fifty dollars (ten percent of five hundred) to bail their son out, his parents decided to keep him in the most violent jail in Philadelphia to teach him a lesson. I hoped his parents felt every ounce of emotional pain they deserved for doing that, for I knew the amount of fear that nineteen-year-old faced. I tried every way to kill myself when I was first incarcerated the night of the robbery, out of pure fear of getting stabbed or raped. I ripped the stitches out of my neck. I swallowed tube after tube of toothpaste. I even saved my orange peels up each day and tried to eat them all at once to choke to death. Luckily, none of them worked but I did succeed in doing some temporary damage to my eyes after trying to scratch them out with the corner of the business card my lawyer's assistant had left with me. My psychotic reasoning was that the judge might go easier on a blind man. After another whole night trying to make the attempt at blinding myself, I couldn't see the morning after. It was only when the nurse came by on her daily rounds and saw the scratch marks on my eyes that the psychiatrist was called. I was given yet another injection.

Fortunately, my eyesight came back by the time afternoon rolled around, and no permanent damage had been done. It still upset me that his parents wouldn't pay his bail, and it made me even more grateful mine did. I don't like to think about what would have become of me if my parents disowned me for bringing "shame" to our family, and after hearing about the hanging, my appreciation for having my family's support grew stronger. The huge stigma surrounding mental illness in the Indian community, as well as the unfortunate level of ignorance, made me vow I would work to reduce both upon my release in the hopes that this would never happen again.

Uncle Fred

Positivity was what continued to move me forward and not dwell on the darker aspects of jail, and sometimes that would come in the form of the kindness of strangers. One of the biggest inmates on my block was a former member of the Aryan Nation named Fred. Covered in Nazi tattoos, he was now a born-again Christian who was adamant about spreading the teachings of Jesus with anyone who would listen (and some who wouldn't). I developed a special liking for Fred right from the beginning of my time on A block. Knowing that I was a fish among sharks, he came up and introduced himself to me.

"Let me know if any of the other inmates bother you, and I'll put a stop to it."

Despite his kind advances, I still didn't imagine fate would put me in his cell six months later.

Fred had a loving family who put plenty of money on his books for commissary. Every week, he would get a big bag full of snacks and share it with me, knowing my parents "only" put twenty-five dollars for me every week. Honeybuns and cheese curls aside, we also spent every day working out together in the cell. He taught me tricks inmates use to put on muscle in jail, as we didn't have access to the weight room at this time.

Despite the love of his family, there were times when an intense wave of sadness came over his face. He explained that, even though most of his family was supportive, his two nieces were terrified by him. They had both seen him go into an intense rage on several occasions (as he often did), and Fred had threatened one of their boyfriends with a lead pipe one time. Although he kept a picture of both girls on our windowsill, they never answered his phone calls, or even wrote back when he tried to contact them. There is something discomforting about seeing a grown man cry, but I had to set aside my feelings of unease on more than one occasion until he would stop.

He treated me like I was his nephew, and I even called him Uncle Fred. I alternated calling him this with my favorite nickname for him, "Special" Fred, since he told me he was in the "special classes" when he was younger, and even rode the short bus. Regardless of my teasing, he looked out for me and taught me who and what to watch out for in order to make it through my sentence. This only made things more difficult when I abruptly moved out of his cell.

I'll never forget the feeling that came over me the day Fred told me he had HIV. Bits and pieces started to make sense. The copious numbers of visits to the doctor, the way his skin was pale, the way he would always talk about wanting to die so he could go to heaven. This made the decision to move out even harder. Things had gotten somewhat tense between us and I was scared I might somehow contract his disease. My instincts told me I would be better off if I were to switch cells.

Fred was saddened by my decision, and we were never the same after that. CO Ford told me I broke his heart, and after he had been so kind to me, leaving his cell was one of the decisions I wasn't proud of. I was still in survival mode, however, and now with my options limited, I knew I needed to find a new cellie. Fast.

Living in a Cell with Carver

Darius Carver was not your typical inmate. He had done over a "dub" (twenty years) in upstate prison; twenty-three to be exact. He was originally sentenced to three to five years for burglary but ended up having a psychotic episode his third year in and stabbed a prison guard. The judge decided to give him "hard time" after that and added twenty years to his sentence. After maxing out his sentence, he was given the typical bus token to get home from the prison. However, he ended up missing his stop and got off in another part of the city entirely. He came upon a house and, either by delusion or on purpose, decided to go in. The family that lived there happened to be home and immediately called the cops. Now he was back in jail for attempted burglary.

I couldn't imagine doing that kind of time in upstate prison, and then not even making it home to see my family. I figured he must be close to his loved ones since he was always on the phone with them.

That's nice, I thought to myself as I saw him once again using one of the jail phones. At least his family is supportive.

When I went to the row of black phones to call my mom, I couldn't help but observe there was something unusual. I noticed there was no regular dial tone, and all the phones were silent.

"What gives?" I asked CO Grayson.

"Phones are down," he said.

Puzzled, I asked him how Carver was able to get through to his family.

Grayson laughed.

"There's no one at the other end of the line, Rohan. You didn't know Carver was crazy?"

Stunned, I stared blankly at Grayson.

"You mean every time he's been on the phone he's talking to himself?"

Grayson laughed.

"He talks to the voices in his head. C'mon, Rohan, weren't you supposed to be a doctor?" he joked.

And with that small revelation, it suddenly became obvious why Carver was on the Mental Health block.

Still, after moving out of Fred's cell, he was the best option I had to move in with that I could think of. After all, we developed a good rapport together, and he hid the fact he was crazy well enough that I thought I could still have normal cellmate conversations with him. Plus, he looked like Dave Chappelle and, like the comedian, was hilarious.

I was mistaken.

The instant I began moving my belongings into his cell (right across the hall from Fred's), I noticed the strong odor of something rotten.

"What's that smell?" I asked Darius, trying not to offend him.

"A rat died in the vent. I filed a grievance to get it removed, but so far, no luck."

I didn't know how long I would be able to last in his cell with the smell of dead rat filling my nostrils. But that was only the beginning of my problems.

During 5 o'clock lock in, I looked forward to just getting some rest. Carver would have none of it.

He began ranting how Bill Cosby owed him three million dollars, and that Oprah promised she would bail him out. Carver then went on to explain how there was a computer chip with a microphone implanted behind his right ear that would feed him all these celebrities' phone numbers, which he would then "call up" to get in touch with them. As I looked at him, trying to hide my chagrin, I could see how dead serious he was.

"Look, here are just some of the numbers I've gotten," he said proudly, showing me book after book of pages filled with numbers.

"But Darius, those numbers are longer than nine digits. They wouldn't work if you dialed them on a phone."

But it didn't matter. He was so lost in his hallucinations and delusions that my remarks couldn't reach him. Evening medication could not get there soon enough, as the CO let us out of our cells. I told T.C. about my predicament, and he suggested I move in with him. Relieved, I asked the CO on duty if that would be ok. I broke the news to Carver explaining to him that I just was not used to the smell, and it was making me nauseous. He said he understood, and I packed up my things with no hard feelings between us.

The next day, CO Jackson stopped me after I had gotten my evening medication.

"I heard you were in Carver's cell," he said, laughing. "You still got your shoes?"

"Yeah?" I replied, confused.

He explained the last inmate who moved in with Carver was brutally beaten, raped, and had his shoes stolen. He went on to tell me the man later died from the assault. I couldn't believe it. Was he just messing with me?

"Good one," I said, laughing back.

As I started to walk away, Jackson seemed irritated that I didn't believe him. He called out to Carver (who was on the phone, of course).

"Yo Darius, remember Brian Gibbs?"

"Oh yeah, didn't he die?" Carver said, laughing.

Still not sure what to believe, I walked away from both who remained in hysterics. If his cellmate didn't survive, wouldn't Darius get charged with murder? And why was he not charged with rape? The whole story must have been made up in order to get a reaction from me. Still, I couldn't help but wonder if I truly had dodged yet another bullet. The feeling that some force was looking out for me only grew stronger.

Going Green

Moving in the cell with T.C. was an altogether different experience. He reached out to me on several occasions when I was in the cell with Fred, offering to cook chi-chi's with him, Ace, and Frank Villano. Since you can order items from commissary such as rice, ramen noodles (soups), cheese, and various toppings (such as buffalo chicken and jalapeno peppers), many of the inmates would get together at evening medication time and "cook." Scalding hot water was provided from a dispenser in the corner of the day room, and it was fascinating to see how creative some of these inmates could be when it came to food.

T.C. and I would chat for hours on many different subjects; everything from ghosts, to sports, to women, and even what we would do when we were back on the outside. As the block representative at the time, T.C. had connections many of the other inmates didn't. He used his connections to try and score some weed, or "green," as it's known in jail. T.C. sold highly valued food items, five dollars' worth in total, to Jorgé who was a kitchen worker. Inmates who worked off the block had the best chance of obtaining marijuana, but weeks had gone by and Jorgé still hadn't delivered on his promise. He asked Buddy to get some as well. Then the day he had been waiting for finally came.

It started off like any other day, with inmates congregating in our cell and cracking jokes. T.C. and I were both getting our day started by drinking coffee and I was pretty relaxed at this point in my jail sentence. T.C. and Ace had helped make my bid really comfortable, and along with the books my mom had been sending me, it hardly felt like I was locked up at all.

Buddy came rushing in and told the other inmates to scatter. When it was just the three of us, he pulled out a "stick" of green, and started rolling it in the white tissue paper that the toilet paper comes in. T.C. checked the doors to make sure the CO's were occupied with other things. When the coast was clear, T.C. took out his batteries and bread twine to light up the makeshift "joint." He took turns inhaling and checking the door, and then put baby powder and shampoo on the vent to cover up the strong odor.

Watching T.C. get high, I started to feel the effects by association. We went out and explored the block, trying to play it cool, but everything was hilarious. T.C. and I were laughing hysterically at everything when we came across an inmate by the name of Toby who remained locked in his cell. He was raving on about how the authorities had shut down Nick's Check Cashing place, which according to Toby was a front for brain scanning operations (he was a paranoid schizophrenic). This was nothing new, but on that day, T.C. and I just lost it. I hadn't laughed so hard in perhaps all my life, and things just kept getting funnier. Luckily, T.C. and I laughing on the block was nothing out of the ordinary, and we didn't draw any more attention to ourselves than we normally did. After our sides hurt and we couldn't take anymore, we retreated back to our cell to eat some commissary.

The food tasted amazing, and I was really enjoying myself when all of a sudden Jorgé came knocking. I barely cracked the door when he came bursting through, excited to share a stick of weed. Jorgé had no idea T.C. was already high, and T.C. and I just looked at each other. He couldn't believe his luck!

Looking back on it, it seems likely that a shipment of green had come into the jail at the same time, which may be why he was able to get it from two separate sources within a relatively short span. Whatever the case may have been, life was good while living with T.C. The time passed by at record speed and, along with the books my mom kept sending me, my sentence became a non-stop party. Around this same time, I read a self-help book which had a quote that Jesus was alleged to have said: "The Kingdom of Heaven lies within you."

My time living with T.C. taught me that this was true. I wrote it on my wall in 49 Cell right above my door as a reminder of the fact that you can be happy despite your circumstances; a lesson I am forever grateful I got to learn.

Learning the Art of Public Speaking

Around the same time I was living with T.C., I took another course called "Thinking For a Change." It was geared towards repeat offenders and how to rewire behaviors and patterns in order to not return to jail. Most of the teachings were very basic, to the point where I found them humorous – don't get high with your children present, don't stab someone because of a heated argument, etc. Of course, I didn't believe I needed the class. However, I felt I could add graduating "Thinking For a Change" to the list of accomplishments I was planning on writing to my judge to convince her to release me on my minimum date. It also felt nice to get off the block twice a week (I now felt more confident leaving A block as a result of taking the "Inside-Out" class). It was a huge class, with over forty inmates registered. Not all would attend every class, and some even dropped out. A few were released or sentenced for their case and couldn't come for that reason.

The only inmate I knew before the class began was my friend Q. Similar to when I was in high school, I would spend most classes hiding in the back and cracking jokes. The difference here was that I was surrounded by inmates, some of whom had committed violent crimes. We were the only two inmates from A block, and we kept to ourselves except for when we were divided into groups and participation was required. One inmate who left an impact on me was named Smoke. He wore a long beard which had turned nearly all white. His eyes had a yellow tinge to them, which made him look downright evil. Smoke had been down for seven years fighting a murder case. Now a devout Muslim, he found comfort in the teachings of the Koran, although he claimed he was innocent of the murder he was accused of committing. Smoke admitted he had gotten away with a lot more out on the streets and it was only a matter of time before it caught up with him. Now facing a life sentence in upstate prison, it seemed crazy to me that he might never be able to use what he learned from the class back out in society, if convicted.

That's not what struck me the most, though. It was the odd calm he had about himself, like he was mentally prepared for the worst and had accepted either outcome. At twenty-four years old, I felt I would be an absolute mess if I were facing life in prison. I couldn't imagine eating or sleeping, yet there was Smoke, raising his hand to participate often and even occasionally making jokes. It was a common theme I would find hard to accept, no matter how many times I saw it. Inmates, for whatever reason, put the impending time they were facing in the background and actually *lived* in jail. Whether it was cooking chi-chi's, cracking jokes, or playing cards, many of them inherently knew how to stay in the present moment and not worry about the future – something I admired.

After nearly three months, the time came to start preparing for our graduation. The teachers asked for volunteers to give a speech at the ceremony. I remember a few raised their hands right away, eager to be the center of attention. I was the opposite. When they called for volunteers, I sank in my chair, hoping to become invisible. Inmates could either give a speech, read from a religious text, or put on a performance as long as it was relevant to the class. One inmate in particular stood out among the rest. He was an older man, bald and perhaps in his early forties, named Terrell. His physique was as big as an NFL linebacker, but he had a lot of wisdom to share with the class. It was apparent he had been through a lot, and this was just his latest stint in jail.

Terrell volunteered to sing a song for the ceremony. He was Christian and wanted to sing a hymn that was very meaningful to him. As he went to the front of the class to display his talents, the class sat ready. What occurred next is still one of my most hilarious memories from jail.

His voice was so high pitched, it pierced the air like a child. Almost immediately, inmates started looking at each other, trying not to burst out laughing. They couldn't help it; it was just too funny. The juxtaposition of such a big, intimidating figure who had the singing voice of a prepubescent young boy was too much for us to handle. I was trying so hard not to laugh, I literally had to bite the inside of my cheeks like I used to do back when I was a kid trying not to laugh at an inappropriate situation.

This isn't high school, Rohan, pull it together, I thought to myself. But it didn't matter. I burst out laughing even harder, now the loudest one in the class. I was terrified of what Terrell might do to me, but I just could not stop. For some reason the more scared I was, the funnier the situation became.

Finally, he finished singing, and the amusement was over. Even the teachers had chuckled during Terrell's performance, and I was impressed he still had the confidence to finish strong despite all the laughter. Still terrified of what he might do to me, I did my best to avoid eye contact.

The teachers asked who would volunteer next. An inmate to my right said, "He should go," pointing at me. My heart sank into my stomach.

"Yeah, make him go!" came the cries from the mob.

"No, I..." I managed to stutter. But it was too late. This was not the first time my wicked sense of humor had gotten me into trouble, but this was by far the most frightening.

As I stumbled to the front of the class, my mind began racing about what I should say. I had no speech prepared for such an occasion and couldn't imagine how this could end well. Finally, something came to me. It was a verse from the Upanishads, a Hindu holy book I read while incarcerated.

"Uhh..." I stammered on. "This is a passage from a Hindu holy book called the Upanishads." I didn't expect to get a standing ovation; I only wanted to make it through so I could get back to my seat.

"Two birds of beautiful plumage, comrades
Inseparable, live on the selfsame tree.
One bird eats the fruit of pleasure and pain;
The other looks on without eating."

My voice quaked so badly, nobody even laughed or made a joke. They just sat there in shock at how nervous I was. As the teachers and some of the inmates gave a slow golf clap, I found my way back to my chair and sat down.

Glad it was over. I didn't say a word or laugh at any of the other inmates for the rest of class. Now that I knew I would be giving a speech at the actual ceremony things didn't seem so funny anymore. The only other noteworthy event was that Q had also been chosen to give a speech. His went a lot better than mine, however. In the jail hallway on the way back to my block, I stayed behind several inmates, one of whom was Terrell. To my surprise, he turned to me while walking.

Shit! This is it. I thought.

"Hey, I really liked that verse you spoke up there," Terrell said. "Just need to be more confident."

"Yeah, I still gotta work on it," I replied. "Thanks!"

What stuck out to me was his friendly demeanor. I wasn't expecting someone his size and with his criminal history to be so open, especially to me after I had so blatantly disrespected him. When I got back to my cell on A block, something was different from the way I used to approach challenges. Despite the fact that I had just given what was perhaps the worst improvised graduation speech in history, I wasn't panicking in the slightest; something in me just KNEW I was going to do well. I had been reading books my mom had sent me which taught me the power of viewing situations in a favorable manner, and the role your attitude plays in determining the outcome of events. I knew that by viewing this as another challenge I would grow from, that is exactly how I would experience it.

Suddenly a thought came from the back of my mind about a book I once heard of called *The Art of Public Speaking*. It was by Dale Carnegie, and if there ever was someone who could have used it, it was me. I excitedly called my mom when I got back to A block and asked if she could order it for me.

"Sure betu[9]," she replied. My mom was happy I was staying positive and loved the fact I wanted to read a Dale Carnegie book. She was a retired librarian and it was because of her that I grew up loving to read books; a passion which was reignited by my time in jail. Once again, she came through for me, and the book was delivered just a short while later.

I didn't have much time before the actual graduation ceremony, and only ended up reading the first chapter. But that was all I needed. The book talked about the fear of public speaking and why many people have

---

[9] Word meaning "son" in *Hindi*

it. It also explained many ways you can get rid of it, and I eagerly took notes. The main point which helped me the most was the idea that if you aren't adding value to your audience by public speaking, then you *should* be nervous! Chances are the audience wants you to succeed and is on your side, since no one wants to waste their time listening to somebody ramble on incoherently. This really put things in perspective, and even though my audience was full of convicted felons, they weren't as intimidating as I had initially made them seem.

The next class, we practiced our graduation speeches again and I wasn't nervous at all. It helped that I had written out a speech ahead of time while in my cell. By the time the actual graduation ceremony came around, my confidence was sky-high. Friends and family of the inmates in the class were allowed to attend, and my brother showed up for support. Terrell sang his high-pitched hymn, and Q read his beautiful poem he had written about growing up without a father. When my turn came, I was more excited than nervous. I got up on stage after my name was called and made my way to the podium in front of a crowd of correctional officers, inmates, and their friends and family members. Even the warden of the jail came to watch. In total, there were over a hundred people, and the auditorium seemed packed as I began my speech.

Getting up in front of all those people and sharing my truth felt incredible. I took away a lot from that night, but mainly that with the right attitude, I could step up to any challenge that came my way. I used this memory when I came out from jail and began public speaking at local high schools and middle schools. Anytime I doubted myself, I remembered I had spoken in front of much more intimidating crowds before and performed well. I was really starting to like who I was becoming, and this felt like just another steppingstone on my way to success.

See it, feel it, be it

"Whatever the mind can conceive, and believe, the mind can achieve."

— *Napoleon Hill*

Aside from the tremendous growth I was experiencing in my ability to face challenges, another perk of taking the class "Thinking For a Change" was that one of the teachers, Mark, was a very inspirational speaker. He would end every class with an affirmation saying that whatever we could conceive in our minds, we could achieve in life. He told us to visualize by first seeing it, feeling it, and then being it.

In college, I loved studying physics, but I had always wanted to learn more about it at the Quantum level. String theory was another topic which had fascinated my young mind, and now with an ample supply of free time, I took this opportunity to study both, as well as various other mysterious aspects of the universe, such as dark matter and dark energy.

An interesting point I learned in jail from these physics books, around the same time I was enrolled in "Thinking For a Change", is that space and time are intertwined. In fact, scientists refer to it as one entity: *spacetime*. The further the distance an object is from you, the greater the time it takes light to reach you from that object. And since there is light still travelling to us from stars many light years away, this means that what you see when you look up at the night sky is quite literally a snapshot of the past. Many of the stars you see in your night sky have actually burned out or at the very least, changed position. But what about everyday objects in your immediate environment?

People get caught up in their circumstances and perceive them as their "immediate reality". Bills to pay, chores to do, that weird cousin of yours who won't leave you alone; all seem to be part of your current state of affairs. But if the stars are a snapshot of the past, isn't your outer reality old news as well? Why feel limited by your "present" circumstances when they are just what have been previously created?

If there is no objective reality (as quantum physics teaches us), what, then, is the present? If you will notice, it is how we feel. Anytime you have a feeling, it is always in the Now moment. Even if you recreate a feeling of something that happened in the past by remembering it, you are creating it now. The future, then, could be considered to be in our imagination. So, see it in your imagination (future), feel it in the now (present) and it will appear as your outer circumstances (past).

"See it, feel it, be it," as Mark would say.

Sitting in a jail cell, I knew this to be true. Feeling trapped in med school, day in and day out, and always visualizing the worst case scenarios, my imagination was filled with what could go wrong. By repeatedly doing this and feeling these scenarios in my present, it was only natural my past (circumstances) would be one of jail. As I looked around at what I had created for myself, I knew that these same laws which brought me to such a dark place could also be the same laws which could take me in the other direction as well.

But what was the mechanism by which this idea worked? If the "see it, feel it, be it" concept is correct, then surely there must be a basis in physics with which to explain it. Was I crazy enough to actually think I could uncover it?

An Idea Begins to Emerge

"To truly understand Ultimate Reality, you have to be out of your mind"

—— *God,* Home with God *by Neal Donald Walsch*

If you hadn't guessed it by now, the answer was yes. It began when, one of the earlier self-help books I read, *The Twelve Universal Laws of Success*, stated you must feel as if what you want has already happened. This made sense to me, as it would naturally help to be able to visualize a goal you wish to achieve. However, the next self-help book said the exact same thing: you must feel it as if it has already happened. Then another. Then *another*. Mark told us that even the Bible has verses related to this idea:

> *"Therefore I tell you, whatever you ask for in prayer,*
> *believe that you have received it,*
> *and it will be yours."*
> *Mark 11:24*

Why were all these self-help books (and Mark) saying you must experience your goal as if it already happened? This set up the first assumption: these books were all telling the truth. Feeling your goal as if it already happened causes it to manifest. But why? If they were all tapping into the same truth of existence, there must be a mechanism by which it operates that had some basis in physics. But how could I uncover the mechanism? Then it hit me: if what these books were saying was true, then all I had to do was *feel as if I already had the answer*, and the answer would come to me! What followed in the weeks after felt like there was a supernatural force guiding me to the answer. My impulses led me to three prominent, yet still unproven, theories. First up: String Theory.

String theory states that if we could zoom in on any of the objects from our four-dimensional world, we would see that they are actually the product of tiny vibrating strings. Furthermore, the properties of the vibrating string (frequency, wavelength, amplitude, etc) determine the properties of the object (mass, charge, spin, etc). These strings are folded up into six or seven (scientists aren't sure which) dimensional objects known as Calabi-Yau manifolds. In Dr. Yau's book *The Shape of Inner Space*, he explains that our universe is what's known as a "Cartesian Product" of the four-dimensional world we are familiar with, and these six (or seven) dimensional intricate manifolds. You might be asking yourself, "what proof is there for such a prediction?". I asked myself the same question, but in fact there actually are some. For one, string theory was used to accurately calculate the entropy of a black hole. The traditional route of deriving the entropy of a black hole utilizes what is known as the Berkenstein-Hawking equation, which uses the surface area of the black hole as one of the variables in calculating it's entropy. Conversely, string theory uses a more geometric method involving the microstates each string can be in and multiplying that number with the total amount of strings within the black hole. When both are used, the same number emerges, giving us a hint that there could be some validity to String Theory.

Secondly, we have what is known as the Law of Attraction. This theory has been around for quite some time but entered mainstream consciousness only recently thanks in large part to the megahit book *The Secret* by Rhonda Byrne. It states that our thoughts aren't merely harmless projections, but that we actually attract to ourselves the essence of what we dwell on. This means it isn't smart to keep visualizing the worst-case scenario in order to prepare for less than desirable outcomes, but rather, the key is to focus on what you prefer to happen, thereby attracting it into your life. This theory is often scoffed at, with the idea of getting what you want by cutting out pictures and placing them on a vision board seen as ridiculous. Yet after reading about it in jail, I felt some resonance with this theory. People told me getting locked up wasn't my fault because I was sick, but I couldn't help feeling like I "attracted" these circumstances into my life by my negative thoughts and constant dwelling on worst-case scenarios. It was as if my fears had come to life, and even though it may have been a psychotic episode which caused them to play out, I was the one who visualized the essence of them from day to day.

The third unproven theory is that consciousness is the primary constituent of the Universe, and all matter is secondary. I first read about this theory in *The Self-Aware Universe* by Dr. Amit Goswami, but a lot of it started to make sense. I also read a book on evolution by the famous atheist Richard Dawkins, and although I agree with most of his points, the idea that consciousness simply evolved over time has many holes in it. After all, there is still no explanation for how a subjective experience could have developed (which is the only thing we know for sure) from raw, objective matter.

The theory that started to formulate in my mind is the tiny vibrating strings that string theory talks about ARE consciousness. Think about it. Anytime you have had a feeling, does it not feel like tiny strings vibrating in unison every time it washes over you? We use it in our modern-day lingo. "That person just gives me a bad vibe (vibration)." Furthermore, it makes perfect sense that in order to manifest something you must feel it as if it already has happened. Feeling a particular outcome causes the strings in the inner-dimensional planes to vibrate in a very specific way, which then triggers the molecules in our everyday four-dimensional world to follow suit. Let's think about ghosts for a second.

Regardless of what our modern science tells us, I believe many people around the world and throughout history still think there is *some* truth to ghost stories. But when is a ghost said to haunt a particular location? It's after some poor soul experiences heavy trauma, like a child who was brutally murdered. After all, you never hear of a happy ghost. And what would heavy trauma indicate if this theory is true? A heavy feeling of trauma means the strings vibrate rapidly. So, what is a ghost then? A being whose death was caused by the rapid vibration of interdimensional strings that were never resolved during its lifetime. So even though the person is dead, the strings *continue* to vibrate within the seven-dimensional Calabi-Yau manifolds. Again, we hear this in our common lingo: "that place gives me a bad *vibe*." To state it another way, the strings in the six- or seven-dimensional world continue to vibrate so heavily that we feel it in our four-dimensional world despite the absence of a living body.

Now let's talk about rituals, and why people perform them. Societies dating back from Ancient Babylon, all the way to modern Christians have at least one thing in common: they all involve rituals of some sort. Wicca, Voodoo, and Freemasonry are also heavily ritual-based practices. Even Neanderthals are thought to have performed rituals surrounding the death of one of their clan. Why would rituals be one of the common threads within many major societies and religions? I always found it silly that a group of grown adults would congregate to perform these ceremonies, though I started to give them credence once I read a book on the rites of Freemasonry. Still, I would often mock my mother when she would make us do rituals for Hindu festivals.

"Just move this candle in a circle three times and you will be protected."

Yeah, right, I thought. This is nothing but superstitious mumbo-jumbo.

But what is a ritual supposed to evoke? A certain *feeling* within the person performing them. Therefore, if the theory that feelings are nothing more than strings vibrating in unison within the inner seven-dimensional plane is true, then maybe rituals do serve an important purpose as they would bring about the manifestation that was desired if felt strongly enough.

I remember locking in my cell early one night to write out the main points of this theory, scribbling the ideas on page after page so I wouldn't forget. It just so happened that my friend Taylor (who had one of the more severe cases of schizophrenia on the block) came knocking at my door. He was trying to explain to me why it was important to rub the fluorescent liquid of fireflies over your body in order to attain superpowers. I placated him by saying this was all very fascinating and he should write it down so it could be published in a scientific journal. As he went off and I went back to writing my notes, a thought struck me: Taylor couldn't see how ill he was, so the theories he was proposing made sense to him. Was I the same way? Was I so delusional that, even though this theory made sense to me, I would be laughed at (or worse, placated) if I were to share them with others?

As Above, So Below

"'What would you not have accomplished if you had been free?'

'Possibly nothing at all; the overflow of my brain would probably, in a state of freedom, have evaporated in a thousand follies; misfortune is needed to bring to light the treasures of the human intellect. Compression is needed to explode gunpowder. Captivity has brought my mental faculties to a focus; and you are well aware that from the collision of clouds electricity is produced — from electricity, lightning, from lightning, illumination.'"

— Alexandre Dumas, *The Count of Monte Cristo*

A book my mom ordered which just happened to come as a package deal with *The Emerald Tablets* (a book I had been curious about since childhood and always wanted to read), was *The Kybalion*, said to have been written by the Egyptian God Thoth (pronounced "Tote"). I still remember reading an ancient Egyptian legend as a kid which explained that Thoth was the God of Wisdom. According to the myth, when he died, the people went into his tomb expecting to find vast treasures beyond their imaginings. After all, it was said he could manifest whatever he wanted on this Earth. Instead, they found it completely empty save for an inscription which provided the secret to life, simply "as above, so below." Upon remembering this legend, I realized it fit perfectly with the theory: As "above" (not *literally* above, but rather what happens above in the "higher" interdimensional realm of strings) manifests what happens "below" (the "lower" four-dimensional world in which we live). Could this be what was meant by this ancient riddle? As I manically told this to one my friends on the outside over the phone, he said he got chills.

"It's definitely creative."

I rejoiced with delight.

"But there's no proof," he continued.

My shoulders sank.

"Don't you get it? My life is the proof!"

I explained to him everything I experienced could be traced back to the feelings I had before they manifested.

"In medical school, look how I felt: scared, guilty (for feeling like I was wasting my parent's money), trapped. And look where I ended up! Trapped in a literal jail cell, guilty (now in the eyes of the law) and scared out of my mind."

I continued, "And why is my life so extreme? What's different about me?"

"Your life is pretty extreme," he admitted. "But what's different?"

"Think about it, I have a *mood "disorder."* That means I feel emotions more extreme than most people. And if feelings are what manifest your reality, it would only follow that my life would be more extreme as well."

"Hmm…"

"Think about it: when my life is good, it's *really* good. And when my life is bad, it's *really* bad. It's like there's no in between with me."

"That part's definitely true. I never imagined you'd end up in jail."

You have thirty seconds left on your phone call – the message which had become so familiar to me by now.

I realized that perhaps this theory was not an actual mechanical description of the structure of reality, but it was too compelling for me not to at least try it out as a working model. By feeling the end result of what I wanted to achieve, instead of worrying about how and when my goal would be accomplished, two things began to happen. One, I noticed I was much happier. And two, the positive manifestations in my life began to accelerate to the point where even other inmates began to take notice.

"How Do You Get So Lucky??"

"Shallow men believe in luck or in circumstance. Strong men believe in cause and effect."

— *Ralph Waldo Emerson*

Since I began defining everything that happened to me as "good," coupled with the gratitude I practiced every night (thanking God for whatever transpired that day, and ending with the fact that I still had all my teeth), as well as visualizing the end result of what I wanted to achieve as if it already happened, my luck seemed to skyrocket. I seemed to always be in the right place at the right time, to the point where even other inmates could not ignore it.

"How do you get so lucky?" I heard from them, over and over again.

My chance to test out the new theory came when I went to get my first job. I was standing in a line of inmates, waiting for the Sergeant to place me somewhere. She told the other inmates "Kitchen" or "Block worker," two of the common jobs. "Visiting room," "Barbershop," and "Law Library" were several others. When it was my turn, she said something I hadn't heard before: "Receiving Room."

"I'm not sure," I told her.

"You're not sure? That's the best job in the entire jail!" one of the other inmates next to her exclaimed.

And he was right. There was minimal work to do, which meant a lot of downtime where I could read my books, a phone which allowed me to call anywhere in the city for free, and I got to eat kitchen food instead of the trays which the rest of the inmates were fed. This meant pizza, salad, and even barbequed chicken on Sundays.

When I first arrived in the receiving room, I was told to sweep up the cells that were there, as well as other menial tasks. There were three workers who were inmates, and I really didn't mind staying in the receiving room. Pernell, one of two other workers, was a devout Christian, and within the first week it got annoying when he kept preaching to me why I needed to accept Jesus Christ as my Lord and Savior and give up my "voodoo" Hindu religion. Timmy worked in the backroom, where he had a TV, his own personal bathroom, and even a dumbbell with which to workout. Again, there wasn't much work, and he was often found sitting in one of the comfortable computer chairs watching TV.

I was late on my first few days to work, and Pernell preached to me about that as well. The last day of my first week, however, I just happened to get to work before Pernell did.

"Sharma, we need you in the back," Officer Gary (one of the two CO's who were in charge of the receiving room) said.

"I thought that was Timmy's job?" I replied.

"That piece of shit was caught stealing back there, so now it's you."

I couldn't believe my luck. Sitting with my feet up, reclining in the comfy computer chair which Timmy was sitting in only a day prior, I could hardly wait until Pernell saw me.

I couldn't stop laughing at the expression on his face. He had more time than me, and if anyone were to get "promoted," he knew it should have been him.

"Where's your Jesus now?" I laughed, needling him after CO Gary explained the new situation. He wasn't amused, and out of our remaining time together, there was always jealousy coursing through his veins. Of course, I was only joking, and we remained cool for the most part. We both knew how fortunate we were to land jobs in the receiving room, and we weren't going to risk losing that by squabbling over trivial matters like who stayed in the back.

Even if I did get to control what we watched on TV....

The Perks Keep on Comin'

"The better it gets, the better it gets."

— *Abraham Hicks*

It wasn't long until they filled the third worker position with a young kid by the name of Jamal. He was hardheaded, which Pernell couldn't stand, but I actually liked that about him. I told him he could be anything he wanted when he got out, and he respected the fact that I was myself. We cracked jokes at work along with the correctional officers, and the time seemed to fly by. He was exceptionally bright, evidenced by his chess skills, and as the reigning chess champion of A block, he gave me a run for my money on more than one occasion. I was starting to enjoy my time off the block, reading about string theory and quantum physics, while taking breaks to do pull ups with Jamal and occasionally even doing some work.

As the worker in the back room, I had first choice of any of the sneakers which happened to come through the receiving room. There were some nice black Iverson's which I rocked for a while, but when they got worn out an even nicer pair showed up at work one day. They were Gucci shoes that were exceptionally flashy and, ignoring my fears of getting beaten up and having them stolen, I rocked those as well. Who would have thought I would go to jail and actually *upgrade* my wardrobe?

In addition to getting first pick of all the new shoes, I was able to watch movies on the computer which the CO's would bring in. "American Sniper" had recently come out, starring Bradley Cooper, and I got a little taste of freedom by watching it with Jamal. I also got the freshest set of "blues" that came straight from the laundry. Last, but certainly not least, I even swiped a pillow which one of the inmates was clever enough to fashion out of sheets. It had been confiscated but I managed to smuggle it beneath my shirt on my way back to the block. It may seem like it wasn't really a big deal, but when you're sleeping against a cold, hard mattress, you become grateful for anything which can make your bid a little more comfortable.

In addition to the Gucci shoes which I wore off the block, Deshaun (who was my cellie at the time) stole a pair of black fuzzy slippers and gave them to me before he left. Now with all I had acquired, I felt I had the most comfortable bid of anyone. Even one of the CO's took notice, as I walked out of my cell one morning with some fresh coffee in my fuzzy slippers.

"You're gettin' too comfortable, Sharma," he said.

Maybe he was right, but from what I learned from the Law of Attraction, I wasn't about to start walking around in fear again. From initially going to the receiving room as a coward, saying I was suicidal to escape to DC, to now working there, I had grown tremendously from that scared, twenty-three-year-old who was initially locked up. With the inner work I had done on myself, it felt like my outer circumstances were reflecting that. I decided to ignore the warning, as I laced up my Gucci shoes and got ready for work.

The Art of Rhyme

I remember reading somewhere that the Greeks, or possibly the ancient Romans, believed that poetry was the language of the Gods. And if you look at today's world, you can see that this is true with the most famous poets of our society: rap stars. After all, who lives more like gods in our present-day culture? Famous rappers have the freedom to do what they want, when they want, with some of them even having legions of fans cheering for them and buying their music. Back in high school, I used to idolize my favorite rap stars, but never in my wildest dreams was I able to picture myself being one of them.

I was wary of writing poetry before going to jail, as my oldest memory of reciting rhymes was not a good one for me. It was back in sixth grade, where our English teacher, Mrs. D, had given us an assignment to write a short story. I had decided to make mine rhyme, since it just felt more natural to me. Even though it was fun for me to complete the assignment, and I was very proud of the end result. My work ended up drawing attention to me which I did not appreciate at the time. Mrs. B was the teacher who taught the gifted students, and so I found it odd she stopped by our class one day. It turned out she came to our class because she had graded some of our papers and liked mine in particular. When it came time to share our work in front of the class, she was adamant that I should go first. Too nervous to even go to the front of the class, I stood up and recited it from my desk. Snickers came from some of the other classmates, most likely for the fact that I had gone above and beyond on my assignment and was therefore seen as a "suck-up". I was more than happy when I had finished, eager to take my seat once again. Although my teacher seemed overjoyed at my little "rap", my young mind began to relate expressing myself through poetry with drawing unwanted attention, and it would be more than a decade until I wrote another poem.

When I was roughly six months into my sentence, my love for poetry was reignited from an unexpected source. I had become cellmates with T.C. as if by synchronicity. He happened to be one of the better rappers on our block. He was also the block rep at the time and was very popular among the inmates. T.C. was a heroin addict on the outside and had been locked up for pulling a string of burglaries in order to feed his addiction. Even though he was a year younger than me, I was still able to learn a lot from him during our brief time of living together. Before he was released to a rehab clinic, we would spend hours excitedly talking about our dreams for when we were back on the outside.

Many of the inmates in jail knew how to rap, and a large portion of them really believed they would make it big in the industry. T.C. was different; his ability to put multi-syllable rhymes together was something I had never heard before. He showed me pages upon pages of various songs he had already written and gave me a detailed description of his album he planned on releasing. This all sounded very exciting, and the thought occurred to me on more than one occasion that I might just be cellmates with the next Eminem.

I made sure to get his autograph the night he left, but a strange thing happened the next day; rhymes began coming to me at an astounding rate. It was almost as if I had absorbed his ability to rhyme via osmosis. I quickly began writing them down, but it felt like the rhymes were coming to me faster than I could transcribe them using the pen and notepad I had ordered off of commissary. I was bursting at the seams with excitement to share my new bars[10] with someone, but it had to be someone who would not judge me for my nerdy background. DeRay was just the inmate on the block to listen.

"Yo, those are hot," DeRay exclaimed after I rapped my new lyrics to him. "You just need to spit them with a little more confidence."

---

[10] Verses in rap music

The same critique that would come from Terrell months later regarding my "Thinking For a Change" graduation speech.

I took his constructive criticism well, although I was still not sure how I would accomplish it.

"Keep writing, you'll get there," DeRay said reassuringly.

As the months went on, my written freestyles became more and more popular. I now had many other members on A block backing me up. I rapped my new bars for just about anyone who was willing to listen. Then one day 8 Ball made an announcement:

"There's a jail-wide talent show, here's the sign-up sheet for anyone that's interested."

Perfect, I thought. What better way for the jail to take my raps seriously than by entering and possibly winning a talent show?

I could hardly contain my excitement at the prospect of winning. I began writing new bars feverously and recited them just about anywhere I went; at work, on the block, even for correctional officers.

One night, after coming back to the block from work, one of the inmates, who they called Scatter, said he saw my name on the sign-up list for the talent show.

"Let me hear you spit something," he said. I could hear the doubt in his voice.

He had also planned on rapping for the talent show and was interested in what the competition would be like. After rapping an old sixteen bars I had written for him, he said he was dropping out. My confidence began to soar even more.

"Just make sure you rep A block for us," he said, walking away.

I was incredibly nervous at the thought of rapping in front of inmates on the other blocks, but I knew what I had to do. At the very least, it would make a good story, I thought to myself.

Rapping at work helped ease the fear. The other workers were from B block, and once I spit my bars I was planning for the talent show, they said they had faith in me. News spread to the kitchen workers that there was an Indian rapper on A block who had entered in the talent show. As the kitchen was right across the hall from the receiving room where I worked, I stopped by on frequent occasions to run errands. They would also come to the receiving room when they had downtime in order to use our phone, as it was free (yet another perk of working there). With only a couple of weeks before the big event, one of the kitchen workers, Jamar, called me in to rap for him.

> *My buzz is on green, your buzz is on teabag/*
> *Threw'm a bean[11], OK now give me three back/*
> *Keep givin' me feedback, as if I need that/*
> *Hottest rapper locked up, where the fuck is Meek at/*

The kitchen workers went into a frenzy.

"He's comin' after Meek now? This dude's crazy."

Meek Mill is a mainstream rapper from Philly. He was also a legend in the jail, with inmates talking about him as if he were a God. He also just happened to be locked up at the time for violating his probation, but he was housed in the jail next door to PICC, known as DC. I was eager to showcase my diss to everyone, letting them know I was not scared to go after the best rapper on State Road.

But it wasn't meant to be.

One day, the jail went into lockdown. An inmate on C block ended up stabbing three guards, and because of the incident, as well as the increasing number of fights in the jail, the warden decided to cancel the talent show.

Although I was disappointed, I also felt somewhat relieved that I would not have to appear on stage in front of the rest of the jail. This did not stop me from continuing to hone my craft, however, and I wrote down any rhymes that would come to me on a notepad I had ordered off of commissary. One poem I wrote in particular became popular, as it made its way around the block. I titled it "Emerald Suppression":

Emerald Suppression

A young woman was running away
From a small village in Bangladesh
Having just lost the love of her life
Her close-knit heart, an untangled mess

---

[11] Slang for "100"

Safa had a child-like innocence
Until now, her life a sack of dreams
Her joy swept away by a river
She felt would never go back upstream

Running, running, not knowing to where
Hoping to mend her forsaken heart
Wondering how life could bring such pain
After her dreams were taken apart

Now tired and at the edge of town
She encountered a curious scene
Having stumbled upon a small cave
Out of which glowed a furious green!

Vaguely recalling she'd been warned
This creature succumbed to her intrigue
Once inside, she saw along the walls
The most wondrous site her eyes did see:

An array of fluorescent murals
Endless and of fantastical scenes
Lines of indescribable beauty
Surely by supernatural means?

Suddenly her gaze met another's
Those of a hermit of elder years
Her heart stopped as his brush ceased to move
The silence too much, she quelled her fears:

"Your art is Divine, I must say so
But if I may ask, how do they glow?"
Some say a smile crossed the old man's lips
He uttered, "My child, only fate knows."

"You asked your question, now I'll ask mine
What plagues you that brings you to my lair?"

She burst forth with ineffable pain
How fate had shown her life was unfair

His eyes grew wide like he had a plan
"Come, you're too young for a heart so sore.
I keep a bottle for souls like you,
Drink my elixir, feel pain no more."

Her mind thought it too good to be true
But her heart felt nothing was amiss
Perhaps blinded by intense longing;
Longing only momentary bliss

Almost at once she downed the potion
Instantly her pain had gone away!
Where there was once misery, nothing
A miracle came upon this day

Tried to smile at the welcome numbness
But couldn't as her heart turned to stone
A coldness worse than death had seized her
"What cruel trick is this??" she yearned to groan

Could not understand what had gone wrong
Why had she been cursed by this new fate?
Without sadness, there could be no joy
But of course she realized this too late

Descending to her personal Hell
She up and vanished without a trace
No footprints, no clues to where she went
Just a firefly about her place

Quickly the old man grabbed for a jar
And with no sign of making amends
Caught the fly to put with the others
And slowly started painting again...

The Power of Affirmations

"Came from the dirt / I emerged from it all without a stain on my shirt"

— *Jay-Z, "Guess Who's Back"*

Many thoughts and ideas came to me as a result of my ability to rhyme, such as dreams of becoming a rap star, or possibly a famous poet. It felt like a whole new world was open to me, however, an insight I acquired related to rhyming came from a self-help book titled *The Power of Your Subconscious Mind* by renowned author Joseph Murphy. In it, he explains the power that affirmations can have in guiding your life, either positively or negatively. An affirmation is a statement you make to yourself with the intention of providing emotional support or encouragement. You can say, for example, "today is going to be a great day" or "I am a valuable person." These can and often are performed in front of a mirror or written in a journal.

Dr. Murphy goes on to explain what is even more powerful than an affirmation is a *chant*, for then the statement has a higher chance of getting stuck in your head. Even more powerful than a chant, according to the book, is when you include a musical beat in the background and the affirmation becomes even catchier.

Suddenly I had an insight: that's exactly what hip-hop is – statements which rappers affirm over a beat. Many people listen to rap music in order to "pump" themselves up, whether it is athletes listening to "Lose Yourself" by Eminem right before a game, or a student about to give a big speech. Regardless of the circumstances, few would argue that listeners of any genre of music use lyrics over beats to get a certain feeling. Often the feeling listeners of hip-hop are trying to acquire is that of confidence. Much of hip-hop music falls under the category of "braggadocio"; rappers basically bragging about themselves in order to affirm positively noteworthy qualities about their life.

Of course, hip-hop can be used to affirm "negative" qualities as well. Ideas about violence, drug use, and disrespecting women are often at the forefront of much rap music. These lyrics can become implanted into the unsuspecting young minds of its listeners and make them more prone to repeat such behavior. Nowhere was this more evident than in PICC, as can be demonstrated by the following story:

I had been working in the receiving room for roughly three months when a new worker came along by the name of Marquis. He was stocky to say the least, and me and him argued on more than one occasion over various aspects of our job. He had been locked up for aggravated assault and had to sit and wait for his case to play out since he could not make bail. He got along with my other co-worker, Jamal, much better than me and I expended no effort in trying to win him over. I often made fun of him through the safety of being in the backroom. We were separated by a glass window he could not fit through. By this time, I had about fourteen months in and so I was not surprised by Marquis' background of violent criminal behavior. He told me and Jamal that he had beat a murder case at the age of sixteen, in which he was being charged as an adult. Now nearly my age, he was used to being in and out of the criminal justice system. I would overhear him speak to Jamal about prior murders he committed (sixteen in all) that he had gotten away with out on the streets. It would have been hard for me to believe that one person could avoid arrest after that many murders, had I not learned a statistic prior to my incarceration which stated that over seventy percent of homicides go unsolved in run-down urban areas, and that is not even counting the ones which go unreported.

It was about this time that a rapper who went by the name of Bobby Shmurda had a hit on the radio titled "Hot N*ggas". It was extremely catchy and earned a ton of radio play on rap radio stations. One of the lyrics to the song was *"Mitch caught a body 'bout a week ago,"* meaning Bobby's friend, Mitch, had just been charged with murder a week ago. Marquis would sing this line at work over and over again, to the point where it got annoying. I knew he was just having fun however, I was also aware of the dangers of repeating violent rap lyrics as if they were sacred mantras. Marquis ended up getting found not guilty on his case, and was subsequently released back into society. It did not surprise me that a week later, he came right back to jail.

This time – with a murder charge.

In my opinion, stories like his are an all too common phenomenon. Young minds that are inundated with these violent lyrics end up affirming the wrong ideas, which then manifest as their reality through their actions. Although they may gain temporary confidence by repeating such affirmations, their subconscious minds can end up working against them in the long run and it may be only a matter of time until the seeds they have planted in their imagination begin to sprout. Could this be part of the reason I landed up in jail also?

In high school, I would go to sleep by listening to a classic hip hop album every night. Two of my favorites were "The Infamous" by Mobb Deep, and "Liquid Swords" by GZA. Surely all those years of growing up listening to violent hip-hop could not have helped my already unstable state of mind. This realization helped me when I was released by learning to affirm the positive in not just what I listen to, but also when creating my own lyrics.

Mental Alchemy

"True Hermetic Transmutation is a Mental Art"

— *The Kybalion*

Yet another insight I gained while incarcerated occurred as a result of learning about "alchemy." The art of alchemy is an old one, whose roots can be traced to that of ancient Egypt, perhaps even earlier. It's commonly known as the practice of being able to transmute base metals into gold, among other equally unbelievable feats often associated with purifying certain objects. Despite being laughable by today's standards, it is still widely considered to be the forerunner for modern chemistry and was even popularized by one of my favorite books which I read after I came out of jail, *The Alchemist* by Paulo Coelho.

Then there are some who believe in its deeper meaning; that this was all a metaphor for purifying oneself, and that venerable alchemists only used this chemical terminology as a way to disguise its truth from the common man. Alchemists were also often persecuted by authorities, who associated this ancient science with the occult, and even sorcery, which may be another reason its verity had to be concealed from the masses. Regardless, some very prominent scientists throughout history have been recorded as having dabbled with this artform, including Aristotle, all the way to Isaac Newton. I knew very   little of alchemy before I began my sentence, but noticed it popped up in several self-help books, the idea being any negative circumstance can be converted into a positive one; the same way you would hypothetically transmute base metals into gold.

I learned early on in my sentence the power of "mental alchemy" and how importantly our perspectives come into play when experiencing an event. Even a minor change in how you view what took (or what is taking) place can have a profound effect on the outcome of whatever situation in which you may find yourself. Because I chose to define what happened in the most positive light possible, that is the reflection which I received back every time.

Learning how to perform mental alchemy came into play with another one of the greatest lessons I learned in jail, the idea that your circumstances don't determine how you feel unless you let them. The story that illustrates this idea best would be when my parole was denied:

I had read quite a few books already which talked about this idea, so by the time I was coming up on my minimum date, I was ready for pretty much anything. I had done almost a year in jail at this point, and my lawyer said there was a chance I could get out early. In my first year I had not only taken three courses, but I hadn't gotten any write-ups (not to mention I was also working). Things were looking good for me until one morning when I was off to work. Officer Omari stopped me and said I had gotten mail. It was from the district attorney's office, so I opened it eagerly. It stated my parole had gotten denied, meaning I now had to max-out my sentence by doing the full twenty-three months. Other inmates I had become friends with started asking me if I was going to be okay. "Of course," I said. I had already made up my mind that morning I was going to have a great day.

And I did.

I hurried off to work not bothered in the least. No tears, no anger, just a smile on my face. One more year left in jail, I thought. And I'm going to make the best of it.

Just like a book I had read about Gandhi, the powers that be had the authority to keep me in jail, but I wouldn't give them the power to control my emotional state.

Similarly, another day that tested my patience was when a correctional officer named Ford punched me in my face... for no reason. I had literally just woken up as he drunkenly stumbled into my cell, and when I sat up to see what was going on... BOOM! He hit me right in my eye. He was angry at my cellmate, Deshaun, for not going to work that morning, and for some reason, decided to take it out on me. He wasn't only a correctional officer, but also a bouncer at a nightclub. He came straight to work from his second job, and I could still smell the liquor on his breath. Once again, I put my foot down and told myself it is still going to be a great day, and it turned out to be exactly that.

I later used these stories to teach the students to whom I spoke at our National Alliance on Mental Illness (NAMI) presentations that all circumstances are essentially neutral. It is only how we define each situation that determines how we feel about it. I may have learned this the hard way, but I wouldn't trade this lesson for anything. If you decide to maintain a positive state of being despite your circumstances, then you are truly free. I decided to define these two situations as a way to toughen me up, and so that's the benefit I received from both. Of course, some incidents were more challenging to "transmute" into a positive than others.

"Clean up in Aisle 3"

The most violent incident I witnessed during my twenty-three months of incarceration left a stark impression on me. It started as a regular day at work. I was in the back room reading one of my books on string theory when, all of a sudden, the door to the receiving room burst open and a man on a stretcher surrounded by a crowd of correctional officers came through. The man already appeared to be in poor condition, leaving a trail of blood. The guards were pummeling him mercilessly from every angle, and upon further inspection, I noticed his head had been split wide open. Jamal and I were on edge in the backroom, as we watched the terrible beating continue.

"Step back!" an officer shouted to us.

Punch after punch was delivered brutally, and I wasn't sure how much more he could take. I had never witnessed such violence in my life, and to cope with the extreme feeling of unease, I laughed as Jamal looked at me.

What had he done to deserve this? I wondered.

I later found out the man had stabbed three correctional officers on C block, which was right across from A block. It housed the elderly inmates, as well as those in protective custody (PC). While the entire jail went into lockdown as officers went to search each cell for more sharp objects, Jamal and I were ordered back to our cells. We climbed out from the window and I looked over into where they had kept the inmate. The man didn't appear to be moving, but this didn't stop the onslaught from the correctional officers. As I exited the receiving room doors with Jamal, there was a trail of blood which we followed all the way back to our blocks. There, it diverged to the C block door, and Jamal and I opened the doors to our respective blocks. I walked into my cell, as the strip search had begun on A block. My cell was last, and I hurriedly told Deshaun what I witnessed. Before the correctional officers got to our cell, the door to our block opened and an officer came through it. It was CO Gary. I was surprised and he went straight to my cell.

"We need you down in the receiving room," he said.

I put on my blue shirt and followed him back. I could tell he was shaken up at what just happened.

"Isaiah is in quarantine for lice, and I couldn't get Jamal off B block so you gotta clean up the mess down there."

"You gotta be kidding me," I replied. We walked into the receiving room, and a mop and bucket were waiting for me.

"Here, put these on," said Officer Deandre, as he handed me a pair of disposable gloves. The room was empty now, save for pools of blood. It looked like I had stepped onto a murder scene. CO Deandre also handed me plastic bags to cover my Gucci shoes. I felt like the Wolf from Pulp Fiction, helping to cover up a crime. I took a rag out to clean up the window where blood was splattered. I scrubbed up wherever I saw drops of red, but a few spots wouldn't come out. That's when I realized the blood had spilled on the other side of the glass; they had beat this man so bad, they managed to splatter blood on both sides of the window.

An inmate who was waiting to be transported back to his block was snickering at me as I continued with the unenviable task. I shook my head back at him, but I knew I had too many perks working at the receiving room to simply quit over cleaning up after what the correctional officers had done. I remembered when an inmate had smeared shit all over one of the cells and Jamal had to clean it up, so this wasn't nearly as bad. I still get chills, though, thinking about how badly they beat that man. What stands out in my mind is that, not only was he not fighting back, he wasn't even screaming. It's the way he silently accepted his fate for what he had done. Like his soul was already gone, and he was just an empty shell. I wondered what happened to him after he left the hospital. Did he survive the vicious assault? And what was the judge going to sentence him to now? I later found out he was mentally ill   but wasn't housed on the proper block due to overcrowding. For days after, whispers went around the jail about what happened. The incident was so sensational it made the newspaper. Perhaps I would never know what caused this man to snap, but all I could do was be grateful for the fact that it wasn't me.

Finding Fearlessness

"Fear is the tool of a man-made devil."

— *Napoleon Hill*

One characteristic I admired from my peers on the block was their level of fearlessness to fight. Even the smallest inmates on the block still had courage to fight the gorillas that roamed around looking to start trouble, whereas I did everything I could to avoid bumping into them. As the only Indian on our block, it was nearly impossible not to attract attention, and if anyone was a target for extortion, it would be a former medical student from the suburbs.

Time and time again, I would see bullies on the block pick on smaller inmates. Yet even the feeblest would put their hands up, ready to fight, if the situation called for it. Before I became good friends with Ace (a twenty-one year old white kid from the streets of North Philly, and one of the smaller inmates on the block), I admired him from afar due to the fact that he put his hands up when Fred (the former Neo-Nazi I became cellmates with, and the biggest inmate on the block at the time) called him out. Fred was tired of Ace messing around all the time and was ready to put an end to it once and for all. Not showing any signs of fear in the least, Ace stood up with his hands balled as if it were a fair fight. It felt like I was holding my breath, when to my relief, T.C. stood up and stopped the altercation at the last minute. When I later asked Ace about that incident, he acted like it was no big deal and said he wasn't scared in the least.

Another inmate who I respected was Deshaun, who I also became cellmates with later. The moment he first came to A block, we all happened to be locked in for dinner. The workers were all out, getting ready to wheel the food cart cell to cell in order to give us our trays. Q, playing around like he often did, yelled out that the top tier wouldn't be getting any food that day. My cellmate Eli and I laughed, knowing he was only joking. Deshaun, whose cell happened to be next to mine on the top tier, didn't think it was so funny.

"Fuck that! Y'all givin' me my food," he shouted.

Q kept up the charade.

"You're burnt[12], top tier. No dinner today, we're short on trays."

Deshaun completely lost it. As he was running down the steps shouting, I eagerly watched from my cell above.

"Shut the fuck up," 8 Ball (who was the Block Rep at the time) responded. 8 Ball had done over twenty years in upstate prison and had no patience for bullshit.

"Naw, fuck that. I'm eatin' today." Deshuan wouldn't let up, and 8 Ball had enough of it. As he also ran down the steps, Deshaun went equally fast towards him with his hands up. Neither were the least bit deterred by the fact that there were several CO's on the block, all armed with pepper spray.

8 Ball was nearly twice the size of Deshaun, but that didn't seem to bother either of them. Deshaun was wearing shower slippers, while 8 Ball had on worker boots.

As the two met in the middle of the day room, 8 Ball's tremendous arm span allowed his fist to strike Deshaun's jaw first. A loud crack could be heard, as Deshaun instantly fell to the floor. But 8 Ball was far from finished. He got on top of Deshaun and repeatedly hit him in the face. I still remember hearing Deshaun's skull bounce off the hard tile floor of the day room over and over again, until the CO's finally decided to step in. They were lenient on 8 Ball since he was the block rep, and therefore didn't write him up for an infraction. That much I expected. What came as a total shock was what happened next.

---

[12] Slang for "not getting what is owed to you"

Deshaun shot up from the floor almost as quickly as he had been knocked down, continuing to shout the same speech he was giving before the altercation.

"Fuck that! I'll get my ass beat, but y'all givin' me my dinner!"

How anyone could take a beating like that and still remain unfazed was beyond me. I became friends with him shortly after, hoping Deshaun's fearlessness would rub off on me. He later told me in our cell that he would've won the fight had he not been wearing shower shoes...

Soon after receiving the letter from the District Attorney's office stating that my parole was denied and that I now had to "max out" my twenty-three month-sentence, I felt oddly liberated. During my first year in jail, I had purposely done all I could to stay out of trouble, even not fighting back when provoked. Every time I had to swallow my pride to avoid a fight, I could feel my self-respect diminishing.

I remember shortly after I arrived, an older man stole my shirt while I was in the shower. When I got out, someone tipped me off to who it was; an elderly man known on the block as "Karate Shawn" (because he was always practicing martial arts in the corner of our block). I didn't care if he knew Karate, I was so infuriated he had chosen to steal from me, I went running down the tier with no shirt on to where his cell was in order to confront him. Even though he gave my shirt back after a brief argument, wherein he claimed not to know whose shirt it was, I felt disrespected. Just about any other inmate would have swung on him, but I knew my family would be devastated if I were to lose my chance of early parole over something so trivial.

The incident with Jabba was another case where I felt like a punk. Even though at the time I was terrified of him and I most likely would have lost the fight, it would have felt good to get in a hit or two, and I knew the other members of the block would have a new level of respect for me had I fought him.

Once the day came where I no longer had to care about getting a pink slip (which is how the jail referred to written infractions), I began behaving a little more reckless than how I spent my first year. I began gambling on sporting events, smoking tea bags more often, and being more involved with some of the grittier members of our block. One of the inmates who I would gamble with was a muscle-head named Nino. He would be the first person the former   me would avoid out in the real world; someone whose shirt looked tight despite the fact he wore a XXXL. As a fully-grown man with obvious anger issues, you could catch him working out more often than not.

Nino disliked me right from the start. I remember watching the local news in the day room with the other inmates who chose to stay out past the first lock-in, when all of a sudden, a story came on about the legalization of gay marriage in Philadelphia. Nino went into a homophobic rant, using the word "faggot" with no restraint. I already disliked him for the fact that he was locked up for hitting his wife, and at this point I had had enough. I had no respect for men who put their hands on women like that, and with no fear of going to the hole or getting written up, I argued back:

"How does them getting married affect you in any way?" I asked.

He returned back with some dialogue about how it was "gross," and went against God.

"Time to lock in," CO Grayson shouted, and we left it at that.

Once football season started, it gave us all a reason to look forward to Sundays besides our chicken dinner. A lot of excitement had been generated due to the fact that the Eagles were doing well. A week or two after my initial argument with Nino, the Eagles were playing the Ravens. Of course, being from the Philadelphia area, I was rooting for the Eagles. Serendipitously, Nino happened to be from Baltimore and was therefore a Ravens fan. It was only natural we would bet on this game, and as our quarterback at the time (Nick Foles) was on a hot streak. I was more than happy to win some commissary off of Nino.

I ended up winning the bet, but Nino ended up going to the hole for fighting another inmate before commissary came that week, and so I couldn't get paid. When he returned to the block a few weeks later, it seemed his anger had increased. As I walked by, he said he hadn't forgotten about our bet and he was going to pay me later that Thursday (six ramen soups), when commissary came in. I nodded to him and went to my cell to do my inventory of what people owed me that week.

I came down from my cell to ask Nino if he could make them shrimp flavored, as I already had a lot of the other flavors coming in.

"Look man, Ima pay you what I pay you," he exclaimed. "You keep fuckin' around, an your ass ain't gettin' no soups."

His words were loud and reached the ears of a crowd of other inmates. Some of these inmates owed me commissary as well, and I knew Nino "burning" me for my soups would set a dangerous precedent.

My mind was made up what I had to do. I would wait for something else to grab his attention, then "steal" him (a term meaning to hit someone when they're not looking). I had seen Ace steal a bigger inmate before, and I figured it would be worth it, even if I got my ass beat.

Unfortunately (or fortunately), I happened to be wearing my fuzzy slippers that Deshaun had stolen from an abandoned cell and given to me, so I walked back to my cell to put on my black Iverson's. Derek (also known as D-Roc, and someone who I kept in touch with after my release), was my cellmate at the time, and asked why I looked so tense. My hands were shaking, and I'm sure even he could hear my heart pounding as I laced my shoes. When I explained the situation, Derek said he was coming with me. Being bigger than me, I was glad to have the help and with the two of us, I figured we'd have a decent chance of winning. At the very least, the other inmates on the block would know not to burn either me or Derek.

We walked down the steps of the top tier, heading towards the edge of the dayroom where Nino sat watching TV. I walked into his view, waiting for him to say something again that would instigate a brawl. Instead, he surprised me by speaking calmly. He explained he just had an argument with Gamma (the new block rep) when I had approached him. He was still angry about it at the time, which is why he snapped at me.

"It's cool," I responded, relieved it didn't have to escalate the way I imagined. Later, when we were in our cell together, Derek and I laughed about the incident. At the end of the day, both of us could have taken a severe beating and gone to the hole for what amounted to only three dollars' worth of ramen soups. Now not caring about any write-ups, it had taken me a year to develop that jail mentality; one that I had to unlearn once I got released.

A Friend in Need

An inmate I had a close connection with was a thirty-year-old named Thomas. He and I connected through our mutual interest in physical fitness. He was a personal trainer on the outside, and we often worked out together. For the most part, Thomas was a positive person, so it surprised me when one day he came to me baring his troubles. He explained how he had just gotten off the phone with his girlfriend, and she decided to leave him when she found out he was locked up. On top of this, he claimed his mother was hoarding his social security checks while he was imprisoned. He would be dead broke by the time his case was through. Not to mention he was going to lose his cat and apartment.

It was at this time I so happened to be reading a self-help book my mom had sent me titled *How to Stop Worrying and Start Living*. It was another book written by Dale Carnegie, and it explained numerous techniques on how to conquer worry. A tip I found to be particularly helpful (one I have to remind myself of to this day) is to live each day one at a time; forget about the past and do what is in your power each day to move closer toward your goals. I thought the book may help Thomas, so I asked if he wanted to borrow it.

"Couldn't hurt," he replied.

As we locked in for evening count, an inmate a few cells down from me started pounding on his cell window. This was nothing new, but the severity of each bang was harder than any I'd heard before. The next thing I heard was the sound of glass shattering. He apparently hit his cell door window so hard it broke. His cell was just out of view of my tiny window, but I could see pieces of the window as they scattered over the top tier. What I didn't see was that one of those sharp fragments land underneath Thomas' cell door.

While I spent the night like any other, listening to the radio and visualizing my dreams of when I would be released, Thomas later told me he was up all night pacing his cell, debating whether to cut his wrists. He told me it was the book I loaned him which saved his life. Glad I felt inspired to let him borrow it. I was fortunate he was still with us.

I learned you can't save everyone, however, and you can only help someone who actually *wants* help. I felt like I could not help some inmates, and therefore did not even try.

I learned the best way to help in those situations is to live the best life you can live, thereby acting as an example for those who may be struggling but still don't want help. That way, they may see how positively you're living and may choose to match that state of being. But if you simply feel sorry for them, or even try to give advice, not only will they most likely not be able to hear it, but you no longer give them the choice by example of what a fulfilling life could be like. It's for this reason I stopped feeling sorry for people, even when I was released. Some may call this lack of compassion "cold", but I realized it doesn't help them and only adds to their misery by validating it. The funny thing is, I noticed when I turned my attention on myself and started living my best life, I found people actually came to me for advice, rather than me having to push it on them.

Unshackling the Mind

"For the One who is pure in his mind, he is free.
At first, I wasn't sure. Now I find that it's me."

— *Rx Mundi*

Whether I could help them or not, there was never a shortage of interesting characters to talk to on my block. It felt like each inmate could have their own megahit film showcasing their life stories. I found it funny that the deepest conversations I had in my life were with convicted felons. The same people society taught me to fear growing up. The same ones the news showed night after night. Yet here they were, my temporary family, embracing me like a long-lost brother. One inmate I became to be close to was Jason, who was there for lighting a shower curtain on fire at the residential home he was staying at. We bonded after I found out he went to college at the University of Pittsburgh, right down the street from my alma mater, Carnegie Mellon. He never graduated due to a psychotic break he had during his freshman year of college. Shortly after, he was diagnosed with schizophrenia and not long after that, he ended up in the criminal justice system.

He aspired to write the next big fiction blockbuster after reading *The Hunger Games* trilogy while incarcerated. Jason would often show me his rough drafts and I would critique them.

I just finished one of my typical phone calls with my good friend and former roommate in college, Prakash, where we would discuss plans for when I got out. I also shared some of my new rap lyrics with him, and we discussed how cool it would be if we made it big in the music industry. As we talked about how he wasn't happy at his job and discussed alternate places of employment, a thought occurred to me. Many people in society are in a jail of their own. Whether it's being imprisoned by their belief systems as to what is possible and what's not, or of their own fears, they remain stuck in a cage of their own making.

I felt I should share this realization with someone, when I saw Jason sitting by himself. I hurriedly walked over to him, fearing there might be another full response/lockdown, and I would lose my train of thought. After sharing my revelation with him, Jason noted that it wasn't too long ago that I was in the same category of being mentally incarcerated. A new thought emerged now, about how jail was actually the best thing to happen to me. I pictured where I would be had I remained in the same state of mind that I began my jail sentence with. Probably stuck in an office, like Prakash, not happy about my job.

"So, it's almost like you had to go to jail to become free," Jason remarked.

"Yeah, I guess you're right," I replied.

We laughed together at the thought it was society that was crazy, not us.

Towards the end of my sentence, I got a "tattoo" to remind myself of the fact that, no matter where I was, my mind was always free. It was a simple dot of ink between my thumb and index finger, but the meaning was profound to me. A common tattoo that inmates sometimes get is a dot within four other dots (symbolizing a man inside a jail cell) to let others know that he served time. However, I got a dot (without the "jail cell") to represent there really were no "walls"; they were all in my head. Fears, doubts, limiting beliefs – all of them would vanish every time I rubbed my tattoo, even years later.

Law of Subtraction

Not everyone took advantage of the opportunities to grow in jail. Tyrone was what's known as a "jailbird"; someone who spends more time locked up in jail than they do free on the outside. Towards the end of my sentence, I had seen Tyrone come back to the county six times in my twenty-three months. Because I worked at the receiving room, I was usually the first to get word of his return and I would go tell the block when I got off work. I felt almost like Paul Revere announcing that the British were coming. Despite the fact we used to laugh, listen to music, play Spades, and occasionally smoke teabags together, I still always felt safer when he would get discharged. He was like a pitbull. You just didn't know when he would turn on you. I had seen him fight, and he was vicious. The first thing I noticed when I saw him for the first time was his arms; so big, they were practically swinging by his sides. To say I was intimidated would be an understatement. I still have the image of him doing tricep dips off the top tier burned into my memory. It impressed me that he was willing to take such a risk, knowing full well he could fall over fifteen feet if his muscles were to give out on him.

Each time he came back to jail, it felt like he was in an increasingly desperate condition. The seventh time, I only heard that he had gotten locked up again, but this time it was for murder. When word got out around the block that Tyrone stabbed someone to death, the other inmates did not seem shocked in the least. After all, he had been one of the most violent inmates, and on top of that, he had serious anger issues. Perhaps I was just naive, but it was just so hard to believe the same guy I used to "bust it up" and "bid" with was a stone-cold murderer. Then I started remembering some of the fights he had gotten into (he was undefeated on our block). I started remembering what he told me about his childhood and being viciously abused. He just seemed tense all the time, like he was bottling up some unimaginable pain — ready to just dish it out to anyone that had a staring problem. Maybe that's why he was always trying to get high all the time.

The most shocking part of Tyrone's crime, however, was that it was our friend Reggie he had stabbed to death (of all people). Reggie — the twenty-nine-year-old you could slap around all day and he wouldn't do shit. Pushing three hundred pounds, I still did not get why he refused to fight back. Of course, this made his bid a living hell at times, as just about everyone had some fun at his expense (including me). He was a gentle soul who loved to sing, yet it was an altogether different tune when he and I would talk alone. He kept telling me he was a piece of shit and just wanted to die. Reggie explained that he smoked crack on the outside and stole from his family to feed his addiction. I tried explaining that doesn't qualify you for the death penalty, but his self-esteem was already too shattered to hear me.

CO Ford was the one who brought the newspaper article in, where Tyrone made it to page 3. The story was that apparently Reggie, Tyrone, Deshaun, Treyvon, and Ghost all met up on the outside (they all lived in the same area) and would smoke K2 together. I later got the rest of the story from Deshaun, who told me that one day Tyrone and Reggie met up alone. Tyrone wanted to keep getting high, but Reggie didn't want him to smoke up all his synthetic marijuana. And so, naturally, Tyrone stabbed him to death. They said he stayed in the house with Reggie's dead body for two whole days before calling the cops to confess. Now he's doing life in prison.

Other inmates would tell me that, even though Tyrone bragged about his lifestyle on the outside, he was really homeless and didn't have anything worthwhile being out on the streets, which is why he kept getting himself locked up. Then I remembered the way he would fondly describe life in upstate prison: the better food, TV's in your cell, a real weight room, etc. Almost like he missed it and still wished he was there, rather than being stuck in the county jail.

The irony hit me that Tyrone's deepest desire was to do life in prison (though he would never admit that), and Reggie's deepest desire was to die, but he was too scared to commit suicide. Did the universe pair these two up, the same way it later did with Tianna and me?

The Importance of Sleep

It was getting towards the end of my sentence, and I was cruisin'. Joking around with my co-workers at my job made the time fly by, and when I came back to the block at night, my friends made my bid much more enjoyable. I would then read until lights out, or "bust it up" with my cellie, DB, telling stories and laughing until our sides hurt. Time and time again I had managed to avoid getting my ass kicked, aside from roughhousing with the inmates, and things were looking good for me. I now had more time in on the block than just about anyone else, and because of all the violence I witnessed, I felt like I had become severely desensitized as compared to when I first arrived on A block all those months ago.

One morning, CO Ford was doing his normal rounds with Solomon following him. There was no real bad blood between me and Solomon, but on this particular day, his childish antics went too far. He came into my cell, and with DB sleeping right above me, started shaking me and slapping my legs and feet. I was unsure what I had done to make it seem as if it were okay to horse around like that, but I was infuriated at the level of disrespect Solomon was showing me. He was still quite young, and it seemed he forgot where he was – he had gotten too comfortable with the other inmates, and now with me in particular. Perhaps it was myself who had gotten too comfortable, but either way, I felt like this time he had gone too far.

I yelled for him to stop playing around, and finally he and Ford left my cell. Of course, in order to liven things up, horseplay was natural in jail. For example, my good friend at the time, Treyvon, had splashed me with water once in the morning, and then ran out of my cell before I could catch him. It was all in good fun, however, and after punching him later, I was able to laugh about it. Even I had gotten in on the fun on occasion. But there was something different about this time. I was not cool with Solomon the way I was when Treyvon had splashed water on me. Treyvon was also the only inmate to write me a letter when he got out. Even T.C. hadn't done that. I was now angrier than I could remember becoming during my bid, and I knew I had to do something.

I was not able to fall back asleep, and after talking it over with DB in the cell, I decided I was going to confront him. I did not care if things escalated; I was so "jailed out" at this point, I was willing to get my ass kicked, as long as it meant he would not do it again. I went out of my cell for morning medication and saw Solomon on the phone.

Should I steal him? I wondered. I had my fist balled up, but I caught a glimpse of the Sergeant making his rounds. Even in my angry state, I knew I would be "drawing"[13] if I were to hit another inmate with a white shirt on the block. Ford would be furious that I had made him fill out paperwork and would probably take away some of my privileges. Officer Omari was the other CO on duty that morning, and he had gone out of his way for me on too many occasions for me to just snap on his shift. If I was going to fuck Solomon up, I knew I had to be smart about it.

As I was walking by the officer console, Solomon had gotten off the phone. I decided to say something to him first, and then see where things went.

"That wasn't cool what you did earlier man, messin' around with my sleep like that. You need to stop playin' around so much." I said, making sure to look him straight in the eye. He appeared to be caught off guard, as if he had done nothing wrong, which only irritated me further. Not sleeping was part of the reason I had gotten locked up in the first place, and things were going so well, I was not about to let Solomon ruin my day with his childish behavior. I had kept all my anger bottled up to that point, venting only to DB, so when he laughed, I lost my cool and shouted at him.

---

[13] Messing things up for everyone; "out of line"

The whole day room got quiet, as Solomon looked at me while getting visibly upset that I yelled at him. The other inmates never saw me that furious before, but I did not care. I was ready to fight at that point, but the CO's were not about to let that happen.

"Sharma, lock in!" Officer Omari barked.

I started walking to my cell, feeling some relief that I had confronted Solomon and not kept everything bottled up. The old version of me would have just suffered in silence, too scared to say anything. But with so much time in, I was not going to let myself get bullied by anyone.

As I entered my cell, DB was still in bed. He asked what all the commotion was about, and I explained to him what happened, as I climbed into bed myself. I was happy the situation had come to a close, and Solomon would think twice before messing with my sleep again.

Roughly ten minutes had passed when all of a sudden, the door came bursting open. It was Solomon and he was fuming.

"You got a problem with me?" he yelled. "We can take care of it right now!"

Still laying in my bed, I was thrown off guard by his intrusion. Nino had also come in the cell, blocking off the only exit. The two were frequently seen together, terrorizing members of the block. This time, it was my turn.

I slowly arose from my bed, my voice shaking. Somehow, I managed to get the words out.
"Yeah I got a problem! You came in here earlier an' messed up my sleep; you can't be playin' around like that."

Suddenly, the complexion on Nino's face changed. He looked confused,

"You didn't tell me about that part," Nino said to Solomon. Solomon looked down sheepishly, but admitted it was true. As big as Solomon was, Nino was twice his size and was also twice his age. And if there was one thing he didn't tolerate, it was horseplay.

After briefly being lectured by Nino on some of the rules of jail, including the importance of sleep, something I did not expect happened. Solomon apologized to me. It seemed strange, as either one of them alone could kick my ass, and neither of them had a particular affinity for me. Once again, it felt like there was some force looking out for me. It also showcased the paradoxical nature   of convicts. Yes, they obviously may have done something wrong to get locked up. But in jail, they still had principles, and morals, and time and time again I saw that what (or who) was "right" prevailed.

In this case, that happened to be me.

Freestyle Fridays

A few weeks before my release, a sudden inspiration came to me and I began talking to other inmates on the block about starting up a weekly rap battle every Friday. Many found the idea entertaining, and there was more than enough support for it. Of course, I was up first, and the first challenger I came across was a young, Middle Eastern man by the name of Hakeem. He actually came at me first, before I even knew there would be a battle. I had just woken up from a nap before we came out for medication time, when he stepped to me with some bars he had written "dissing" me. Still wiping the crust from my eyes, and barely listening to what was being said, I was overjoyed I would have the opportunity to display my talents.

I could sense that Hakeem was jealous of me shortly after he came to our block. Although he would never admit it, I could tell he admired the way I was able to befriend people on the block, and that I really had no enemies at this point in my sentence. Conversely, Hakeem had a much tougher time making new friends due to his cocky personality, as well as his penchant for lying. The first week he was incarcerated on our block, he had attracted some unwanted attention from two of my close friends, Jalen and Zaire. They noticed his nice pair of Jordan-brand sneakers, and cornering him in his cell, proceeded to beat him until he gave them up. The black eye he received had him walking with his head down in sheer embarrassment for weeks after the incident.

Within no time, I had a response for his "diss", and I could hardly wait until that Friday to embarrass him even further. A large crowd gathered towards the end of our medication time around the dining area, with me and Hakeem at the center of the circle. I spat punchline after punchline, with the inmates surrounding us going into a frenzy after each one. I could tell Hakeem was thrown off by the cleverness of my ability to make him look foolish through rhyme, and with each bar, my confidence began to skyrocket. The entire battle reminded me of the movie "8 Mile", which was the story of how Eminem gained popularity by winning rap battles in Detroit.

Every one of my punchlines appeared to be a hit, so when I came upon one that had the crowd did not understand, I was thrown off by their reaction. Suddenly the entire momentum of the rap battle shifted. When the time came to vote, I was stunned that the audience said Hakeem won. This taught me a much-needed lesson I would carry with me when I rapped during my presentations for NAMI at high schools and middle schools: *you're only as good as your last line.* It also taught me that the best punchlines (or at least the ones that got the most cheers from the crowd) kept things fun and simple and didn't go over the audiences' head.

I used what I learned in my next battle, which was against my good friend Jalen. He was a favorite of many of the more "powerful" members on the block, despite the fact he exchanged fists with Gamma, the block rep. After the fight, both respected one another, and Gamma even showed up at the battle to showcase his support for both of us. This time, I made sure not to include any lines that may be viewed by the audience as ambiguous. Since Jalen and I were friends, he decided to give me a preview the day before the battle and shared some of his lines with me. Now knowing he was going to use some typical stereotypes about Indian people in his diss, I came prepared with several responses which the crowd viewed favorably. When the time came to vote, I won by a landslide, and me and Jalen shook hands.

Despite my time in jail coming to a close, there was still one last battle I had yet to face. And this time, it was not with words.

The Path of Least Resistance

It was nearing the end of my sentence and I was "jailed out", to say the least. I had witnessed so many fights up to this point, so it is no surprise when I became involved in one myself. I was enjoying my time in 50 Cell, with my cellmate DB. We had developed a strong bond; cracking jokes, rapping while he made a beat against the metal part of his top bunk, as well as cooking chi-chi's. Our cell was up against the barrier that separated us from B Block, and we would often bang against the concrete and shout at our neighbors to fuck with them. Pretending we were off our meds and insane, we could hear them cursing us out and threatening us through the wall. We experienced a lot together in that cell and had each other's back.

When we got a new neighbor who moved next door in 49 Cell, I was ready for pretty much anything. He was one of the younger members on our block, and he looked pretty similar to the rapper Soulja Boi. He often walked around with no shirt, and this exposed the cornucopia of tattoos covering his entire body. Claiming to be in a gang in South Philly, he was the type of character the former me would be the first to avoid on the outside. He had a thick African accent, and we would often see him on his Muslim prayer rug. I had no desire to reach out to him whatsoever. One day that changed.

It was early one evening, when DB and I heard him rapping through the vent during the time we would normally take a nap. My head was pounding from an oncoming migraine and I knew something had to be

125

done. I peacefully asked him through the vent if he could keep it down.

"Pussy ass n*ggas" he now rapped into his lyrics. DB and I looked at each other, baffled, while he carried on. I knew he was talking about us, but he would not say so directly. I tried to explain to him that I was having a migraine and that this was an adult jail, so he needed to be considerate of those around him. He threw more sneak disses*[14] into his rhymes.

"Bitch n*ggas" was the response, and I was infuriated. The one thing I couldn't tolerate was when a migraine came on full force, and the clock was ticking on this one.

"Alright, I got something for ya." I yelled back through the vent. I looked over at DB and gave him the nod. Lacing up my shoes, my fight instincts surged.

When the correctional officers called us out for our evening medication, he was downstairs watching TV in the day room. I knew this was my chance. Walking down with DB, I told him to go left while I walked towards the young kid, so he had nowhere to run. So much anger had been building up, and when I walked within striking distance of him, I smacked him with the back of my hand. The sound was so loud that the entire day room stopped what they were doing to turn and look. Stunned at what had just happened, I quickly grabbed his arms while he remained sitting. Now it was DB's turn, and he smacked his face twice.

"You gonna keep talkin' shit?" I yelled, "or you gonna be quiet now?" I felt no remorse for how hard I had hit him and when I finally let go of his hands, he sat quietly. DB and I walked away, as the inmates in the day room went back to what they were doing. I walked towards Gamma, who was the block rep.

After explaining to him the situation, Gamma said I did the right thing.

"A kid doesn't get very far acting like that in a grown man jail."

The CO's stared at me as I walked to get my medication, hoping the nurse would give me some Ibuprofen for my migraine.

"Damn, what happened to you Sharma?" CO Grayson said. I did not have an answer, but now felt like something inside of me had changed. I had witnessed so much violence during my sentence that it now felt like it was a part of me.

---

[14] To talk negative or degrade someone anonymously

Weeks went by, and I didn't hear a sound come out of him. I felt bad for what I had done and attempted to make peace with him by sliding an oatmeal cream pie underneath his door.

That was a mistake.

As is often the case, kindness gets mistaken for weakness, and this led to him venting his frustration one night after medication. He went on a rant about a variety of topics, but when he threw in the term "7-11", he suddenly caught my attention. It seemed odd to me that he kept refusing to mention me directly, and only offered "subliminal" threats (talking about how out on the street he would have his AK[15], etc). Yet when I confronted him and asked if he had a problem, explaining that we could go to the "projects" and figure it out, he claimed that there wasn't.

As the CO's locked us in for the night, I knew what I had to do. I told DB I would explain the situation to CO Ford first thing in the morning, as he was the only CO who let inmates fight out their problems.

Morning came, and as CO Ford went into each cell to do his typical inmate count, I explained to him what occurred the night before.

"OK, hang tight Sharma. Let me get the youngin's side of the story."

He unlocked 49 Cell and let him outside. He then asked him directly what his problem was. Instantly he went into a rant, and I could tell how much frustration had been building up inside in the weeks prior. He made sure to include the fact that when I smacked him weeks earlier, blood had come out of both the inside of his mouth and nose. He then made some comments about DB, who was awake and on the top tier, implying that he was homosexual.

But something strange happened next. When CO Ford explained that the yard was open (meaning we were free to fight out the situation and resolve it that way), 49 Cell[16] suddenly got quiet and refused. I didn't understand; how could you be willing to defame someone, even going so far as to claim my cellie was gay, but then not want to do anything about it? CO Ford told him to go back to his cell.

"You feel better?" CO Ford said, turning to me.

---

[15] Short for AK-47

[16] We did not bother taking the time to learn his name, and thus only referred to him by the cell he lived in

"No." That didn't appear to resolve anything, and in the process of giving his side of the story, 49 Cell had only made me angrier.

"Well, his cell's open."

"Say no more," I replied.

Running up the steps to the top tier, I got to his cell. Now with the greenlight from CO Ford, I opened the door and burst inside. He happened to be on his Muslim prayer rug at the time.

"Get up pussy, you know what time it is!" I came barreling towards him, full speed.

He swung and his fist hit my upper lip as I closed in on him. We began to grapple, and feeling his strength match mine, we tumbled to the floor. As we picked ourselves up, arms still locked, I was able to free one of my arms and began elbowing him in the back of the head repeatedly. With my other arm still tied up, it was all I could do, but it seemed to be enough as he cried out for the CO's help.

Within minutes from when it began, CO Ford and CO Hawkes came bursting in to break it up. My upper lip was starting to swell, but I felt better now that I felt we were even. In my remaining time while incarcerated, he kept quiet, and I felt like I had done what was necessary in order to maintain the status quo.

Growing up, my parents instilled within me that all violence was wrong. Now with only a short time until my release, there were no remnants of that idea remaining. I saw how violence could be necessary in certain situations and could be used to solve certain challenges. Was I wrong for fighting him? Perhaps. But after reading books on evolution and quantum physics during my bid, one thing that became apparent about nature was that it seemed to always flow in the direction of the path of least resistance. Sure, I could have let the young kid "chump" me and not fought him. I could have spent hours trying to reason with him and teach him a lesson that way. But in this case, the path of least resistance was to just smack him, right?

It would take me years after my release to realize I was only trying to prove my "toughness" to myself. People often make decisions to impose their will upon someone when they, themselves, are afraid. And therefore, a decision to smack someone and then later fight them is not one of power, but actually one of feeling powerless. I was afraid that if I let certain actions slide, my bid would stop being so comfortable. I was afraid if word got out that I allowed myself to get disrespected to such an extent, even though I only had a short time left in jail, it could quickly turn into a nightmare, as I had seen it become for other inmates. As silly as it sounds now, I was even afraid of what I would tell people when I got out of jail, worried about my image and "reputation". But even though I know now I acted out of fear, I don't continue to judge myself for this. What I learned is that we all do what we can in the situations we are in, and the best thing we can do is learn from those choices and move on. Would I make the same choice knowing what I do now? Probably not. What I will say is if I ever see him again, I didn't need to give him that oatmeal cream pie either.

Philly Criminalizing Mental Illness

Now having done the most time out of any other inmate on the block, CO Ford decided to make me the alternate for the Block Representative. My duties were to take the place of the block rep, who was Gamma at the time, if he couldn't make a meeting with all the other block reps and the warden.

The only meeting I ever ended up attending left a stark impression on me. There were roughly seven of us sitting around a table, with the warden of the jail at the head. The other block reps were complaining that, due to overcrowding on A and K block, mentally ill inmates were being placed on their blocks. They were not showering, starting fights with the other inmates, and just being a nuisance in general. The warden then said something that struck a chord with me. He explained that due to mental health institutions being shut down in the area, Philadelphia had essentially criminalized mental illness. There was an overflow of mentally ill inmates, and the jail no longer had the resources to house them properly. This is partially what led to the three guards getting stabbed by a mentally ill inmate, who was housed on the wrong block (he was placed on C block instead, the block for the elderly).

Shortly after that, the warden decided to cancel the talent show I had been preparing for. I just had to trust that this was in my best interest somehow. Who knows? Perhaps I was not ready to perform for the jail under such extraordinary pressure, and the warden had done me a favor by saving me from being booed off stage. If that were the case, my self-esteem was saved.

"King of the World" ... Sort of

On the day of my release, I could hardly believe it. 23 months had come and gone, and I was no longer the same person I was when I entered PICC. I had become much more confident, and now age 25, I felt like I was ready for anything My first week out, my brother helped celebrate my release by taking me to a concert. Drake was headlining, and I'll never forget the feeling of being amongst a crowd of civilians after being incarcerated for nearly two years. It was almost overwhelming, but I was having too much fun to care. Next up came studying for my GRE's. I thought I would apply to graduate school to get my Master's in Psychological Counseling but decided at the last minute it was not the path for me. Instead, I began speaking at high schools and middle schools for NAMI, sharing my story with students as an example of what happens when you don't speak up and get help for your issues. There, I was even allowed to rap at the end of my presentations and get subscribers to my YouTube channel under the rap name, "Rx Mundi."

I wanted to use the name "Rex Mundi," as it means "King of the World" in Latin. However, I was disappointed to find out another band had already taken the name. Once again, fate was on my side, however, as I realized I could change "Rex" to "Rx" – the symbol for prescription medication. Was I king of the world, like I so often felt in my manic states? Or was I simply a madman who was delusional? I left it up to my audience to decide.

The students would sometimes go into a frenzy after I would rap. Sharing my story of recovery in front of an audience gave me more confidence. I was even asked for my autograph on occasion by some of the kids, or to get my picture taken with them. The feeling that I was a celebrity was interesting, since the reality was that I was living with my parents and surviving on SSI. I was okay with that, however, as I had learned from my time in jail that it is the feeling that counts.

"You Are Not Alone...?"

"The worst loneliness is to not be comfortable with yourself."

— *Mark Twain*

An insight which came to me during the months following my release had not occurred to me before. It was the idea that many campaigns use "you are not alone" as their slogan for overcoming challenges. There is something comforting in knowing that others have gone through what you might be struggling with, whether it be battling a disease, conquering a particular fear, or just trying to overcome the challenges life may present you with.

Of course, I think the intent of this saying is fantastic. However, I think we must supplement this message with another that I think is just as important; being alone is one of mankind's biggest fears. It is at the root of many other fears we might not associate with it. For some, it can even feel stronger than our fear of death. Whether this is true for you or not, many people (especially those that went to public school) would agree that fitting in is a pretty big motivator for us, and often holds us back from some of the more wonderful opportunities in life. The issue really is that by constantly reassuring ourselves that we are not alone, we are also fueling this fear that has already dictated too much of our lives. It's implying that there's something *wrong* with being alone, which is only going to make it harder for you if you should someday happen to wake up in that situation. I completely understand that the is no more important time than childhood for reassurance of not being alone. Even losing your kid at Disneyland for an hour can be traumatic enough to leave them with abandonment issues for a lifetime, if left unresolved. But it's also important to let your kids know that it's OK to be alone, so if an emergency occurs and you are separated, they have a set of skills to prevent panic. It also encourages them to express themselves in more fearless ways. Standing out in a crowd can ironically bring up feelings of loneliness too. Such feelings arise from a distortion in the belief system. Loneliness does not have to result from being alone.

Avoiding loneliness has been a recurring theme in my life, as I'm sure it is for many. Back in high school, even though a part of me would rather stay in on weekends than hang with my friends, I often gave into the fear of being alone and chose to hang out with them anyway. Once in college, I caved in to that fear regularly as well, resulting in me not having much time to myself. It also started a pattern of substance abuse, and as is often the case with people who habitually get high (no matter the substance), it tends to start a cycle self-ha of self-hatred. I could not even stand looking at myself when I was out on bail, asking my parents for money so that I could secretly buy alcohol in an attempt to drown out my thoughts of suicide. But once my twenty-three months of incarceration began, and when I finally got time to be myself, a strange thing started happening; I began liking the person I saw in the mirror. Suddenly, being alone was not so bad. The one thing I had feared perhaps most in my life became one of my biggest blessings.

One of the most important lessons I learned in life, which I carry with me to this day, is this: if you happen to be in a room full of intimidating looks (whether in front of an audience of snickering high school students, or on a block of the most violent jail in Philadelphia) you can always count on your reflection to smile back. *Always.*

Stranger Things

"Truth is stranger than fiction."

— *Mark Twain*

By far the most incredible incident of my life (to date) occurred in the Fall of 2015, roughly seven months after I had been released from prison. Similar to Napoleon Hill in his book *Outwitting the Devil*, I am not insisting you believe my account of what happened. I am sharing it with you because, as I tell the students who hear my presentations, if you are genuinely excited to share something, then there will always be somebody out there who will appreciate what you have to share. It also may help others who have had strange experiences find the courage to come forward. And besides, what do you have to lose when everyone already thinks you're crazy?

Several months after being released from jail, I was living back home with my parents and had come across a self-help guru by the name of "Bashar" on YouTube. Darryl Anka (who is the cousin of singer Paul Anka) appears at first glance to be a pretty laid back, normal guy. However, his personality shifts dramatically when he channels the being known as Bashar. For those of you who do not know what channeling is, it happens when a person serves as a medium for another entity. In this case, Bashar claims to be an extraterrestrial from the future who speaks through Darryl. He uses humor and wit to deliver teachings of self-empowerment, and his message that we create our own reality resonated strongly with me.

There were several other of Bashar's teachings which attracted me to him. For example, he teaches that your world is like a mirror, and reflects back to you your own state of being. Get happy first, and your circumstances will reflect that. I felt this to be true from my time in jail. It appeared to explain the many amazing coincidences which allowed me to live so comfortably there. Yet another teaching was that there exists seven dimensions (Bashar refers to them as "densities") which is in line with what the Kybalion teaches. This explains the seeming anomaly that there is a six to one ratio of matter to dark matter in the universe. His main teaching, however, is actually a formula: act on your excitement to the best of your ability every moment that you can, taking it as far as it can go until you can take it no further, with absolutely zero insistence on a particular outcome while remaining in a positive state no matter what happens. He states that this is not just a "nice philosophy," but is an actual instruction manual for the way life works, as excitement is the body's physical translation of the vibration of your Higher Self.

Another channeler I came across was Esther Hicks, who channels a being known as Abraham. She has appeared on Oprah, as well as other syndicated shows, to deliver information regarding the Law of Attraction. She offers several guided meditations on YouTube, and one of which attracted me was designed to bring about financial abundance by clearing up resistance. An old friend from high school, with whom I had not spoken in quite some time, sent me a text the same minute I finished doing the meditation. He said a mutual friend of ours, to whom I hadn't spoken in over a decade, was in town, and suggested the three of us should meet up. Thinking this was the Universe giving me a sign, I immediately said yes. When the three of us met up, there was a synergy in the air which was palpable. It happened to be the night of the super moon, and I felt some strange force was at work. I was not taking my mood stabilizer and antipsychotic medication at this time (I was not excited to) and was only sleeping every four days due to abusing my prescription Adderall. Even though I was completely manic at this point, I was still able to hold normal conversations and keep it together.

Ethan, who was the friend I hadn't spoken to in over a decade, now owned a bunch of startup companies, and after hearing what I had been up to, suggested that I come work for him. Within a week of the three of us meeting up, I moved into his house in Bethlehem, Pennsylvania. It was huge, and he told me he recently spent eighty thousand dollars renovating it. I felt like I was living in a five-star hotel, and Ethan generously told me I did not even have to pay any rent (talk about financial abundance!). The Friday I moved in with him, something told me to go out to dinner on my own, and so Ethan dropped me off at a nearby Chinese restaurant in town. I spent the remainder of the sixty dollars my dad had given me before moving in with Ethan. With no cash and no sense of direction, I walked through the streets of Bethlehem, PA, where I felt like I was in a lucid dream (which is what Bashar says we are living in — physical reality is a dream your Higher Self is having). My cell phone was almost out of juice, and I had no charger and no idea where I was going, or how to get back to Ethan's house. Yet with all this recklessness, I was not worried and felt drawn to walk around. I came across a library and felt compelled to go in, like I was being pulled there on a string. I sat down and closed my eyes, and when I woke up the library was closing.

A Curious Encounter

"And then there was that night, when it was shown to me
What was always in plain sight, but few will ever see"

— *Rx Mundi*

A man who was not there when I closed my eyes caught my attention as he sat staring straight past me. He was an elderly Caucasian man and appeared homeless, but with a wooden staff. Something told me I needed to talk to him, and so I asked him for directions in order to strike up a conversation. We began talking and walking the streets of Bethlehem, where he led me to a nearby McDonald's. The man was absolutely hilarious, but somehow even more wise. This reminded me of someone, but I just could not put my finger on it. We talked some more about topics such as metaphysics and self-empowerment, and the conversation was naturally heading towards the teachings I had recently been learning. I used the phrase "permission slip", something Bashar defines as "any tool, any object, any ritual which gives you permission to be more of who you truly are," playing it off as if I had invented it.

"Oh, so you listen to Bashar also?" said the man.

How the fuck does this random person know about Bashar? I thought, and as if reading my mind, he got quiet and stared at me.

Holy shit! It's *him*! I thought. I was not sure how, but it became obvious to me at that moment that all the synchronicities that had occurred in the weeks prior (meeting up with Ethan, moving to Bethlehem, the super moon) were merely stepping stones to get me to meet this man who I thought was a parallel incarnation of Bashar that night. When he opened his mouth next, the entire energy of our conversation shifted. It had become much more serious now.

After talking further, it turned out not only did he know exactly who I was, but he even knew intimate details about my life (including thoughts that I had which I never told anyone about), as well as who my family and friends were. All this may seem hard to believe, given I had never met him before in my life, but he told me many things that night which I will never forget. He also performed several "miracles" which I was convinced were not mere chance.

For example, there was a newspaper on the table of the McDonald's we were sitting. During the course of our conversation, he used a particular phrase, and when a homeless lady came up to us and handed us a spiritual pamphlet, he placed the pamphlet next to the newspaper which, when combined, revealed the phrase he had just used.

"Now what are the odds of that?" he asked me. Of course, the odds were ridiculously low, and this had me convinced he was a higher density being who knew some sort of magic. He then explained to me that he was able to perform these seeming miracles because there was a "behind the scenes" to this reality which I was not seeing, where things are orchestrated first and then play out in our everyday world.

Regarding metaphysics, he explained that every moment is just the same one moment, but from a different point of view. My head felt like it was going to explode; so much advanced knowledge… and here he was sharing it with the likes of me!

Regarding jail, he told me I had been "protected" during my sentence. This may sound far-fetched, but it actually made a lot of sense to me as there were so many close calls where my bid could have turned violent, but I seemed to be miraculously saved at the last minute every time. It literally felt like there was some higher force out there which was looking after me, and what he said appeared to confirm that. Why had I not been extorted, like many of the bigger, stronger inmates? I was a seemingly easy target and couldn't really explain why I had been given a "pass" by many of the more negatively intentioned inmates. How else could a nerdy Indian former medical student make it through 23 months in the most violent jail in Philadelphia? While wearing Gucci shoes, no less!

I was thinking back to the idea I had come up with while incarcerated, related to string theory and the law of attraction – the concept that these tiny strings were consciousness, and that you can manifest what you visualize by feeling it as if it had already happened. Before I could even ask him about it, he blurted out, "you didn't come up with that! It was *given* to you."

Although I have to admit my ego was a little sore, again, this made a lot of sense to me. It explained how I was able to seemingly connect all these "random" dots, when my lower physical mind had little knowledge of any of these topics at the time. It definitely felt like it was being "fed" to me from a higher source. He also explained to me rituals can be extremely powerful tools, and that I shouldn't laugh when my mom would perform them at home.

Many things remain hazy in my memory from that strange night, however, one thing he said remains burned into my mind to this day.

"Always remember, you have to walk a very thin line," he said, almost as if it were a warning. What did he mean by that? I wondered.

I spent the entire night chatting with this strange being, and when morning came, we ended up at a McDonald's again, but a different one from when the night started. He gave me cash to purchase a coffee and a chocolate chip cookie, and we sat down together to talk. He had me laughing so hard, but within the next instant, he disappeared out the door before I could even get a chance to say goodbye or thank him. The workers at the McDonald's saw me laughing and crying, and due to my strange behavior, called the police. When the police showed up with an ambulance, I was still trying to process what had just happened to me that night, and so my answers came out disoriented. They took me to a hospital in Bethlehem, and from there, my parents came and took me home.

Things Get Stranger Still

Soon after, everything began falling apart. I was in and out of the psychiatric hospital eight times within the next six months. I was still in shock at what had occurred, and I didn't tell anyone about that incredible night for nearly half a year. When I did finally open up, it was to my mom at first. She insisted I was delusional and hallucinating from not taking my medication. Was he merely a fabrication of my imagination?

In all my wildest delusions, I had never made up an entire person before and spent the night walking and talking with them. Also, if he was imaginary, several things did not add up. For one, how was I able to purchase the cookie and have coffee at McDonald's when I had literally no cash on me? It was he who had given me the money for those things, and secondly, even my mom had seen a hoodie he had given me during the night when it got cold. Where could I possibly have gotten that from? Last, and perhaps strangest of all, the book he had handed down to me on pdf format on my laptop remained there. "The Sufi's" by Idres Shah; what did it mean and why did he keep bringing up this mysterious sect throughout the night?

Questions plagued me, and I knew I needed answers. I had no one who believed my story, and the frustration of not knowing what that night meant became overwhelming. I came across another channeler by the name of Rob Gauthier, who does sessions for people by channeling what he claims is a fifth density being by the name of Treb Bor Yit Ni. During our Skype session together, Treb explained to me that the man was not a parallel incarnation of Bashar, but rather, he was a portion of my Higher Self who came down in physical form in order to act as a mirror for me. As ridiculous as this sounded, I had to admit it made sense to me. How else could he have known such intimate details of my life? This explanation also explained why his demeanor changed depending on how I was feeling; he was reflecting back to me my own state of being.

Feeling like I had received some closure on the subject, I was able to finally relax. Months later, while listening to an old Bashar transmission on YouTube, he said something very peculiar which stood out to me and seemed to tie everything together. The transmission was regarding changes in energy that were taking place on Earth, especially during the 2010-2015 time period. Bashar explained that this was a highly accelerated time period for manifestations, and I felt like this was true; my experiences with D.M.T., my manic episode, the time I spent incarcerated, and now meeting my Higher Self had all taken place within this time period, with my journey to Bethlehem occurring in November of 2015. But it was what he said next which made my jaw drop. He said during this time period if you follow the formula of acting your highest excitement every moment that you can, taking it as far as you can until you can take it no further, with absolutely zero insistence on a particular outcome (which I had indeed been doing), "you will, well maybe even quite literally for some of you, be beside yourself."

A smile came on my face, as I realized it was a pun and that is literally what had happened. I remember listening to that same transmission before moving to Bethlehem and not knowing what that meant. After all, you could be beside yourself with joy, excitement, and other emotions. But how could you be *literally* beside yourself? My Higher Self coming down in physical form to meet with me meant that I was actually beside myself,

What a clever bastard.

I felt like my experience had been completely validated.

Outwitting the Devil

"The time people spend in fearing something would, if reversed, give them all they want in the material world and save them from me after death"

—— The Devil, *Outwitting the Devil* by Napoleon Hill

Not everything was candy and rainbows while living in my parents' house after being released from jail. An incident occurred during my first psychiatric hospital stay which I will never forget.

As mentioned previously, a quote that helped me get through my time in jail was something Jesus was alleged to have said: "The kingdom of Heaven lies within you." Of course, the corollary to this is that Hell does too. The first time I was involuntarily committed to a psych ward, I ended up at Lower Bucks Hospital. In some ways, a psychiatric hospital can be more frightening than jail, depending on the delusions you are having. The reason I was involuntarily committed (or 302'd as it's referred to in Pennsylvania) was that the night before, I had woken up at 2:00 in the morning, and in a delusional state, I thought I had to cut off my phallus and consume it. Luckily, fate was on my side and my mom had woken up (as she often does in the middle of the night) and caught me with the butcher knife in hand.

"Rohan, what are you doing?" she screamed.

"I have to, mom. It's the only way." I said, almost as if I were in a trance.

"Anil. Get up! We have to take him to the hospital."

The thing about delusions is that, while you're having a delusion, you cannot see that you are in one. I was convinced that I was in Hell for doing something unforgivable, and the only way to get out and redeem myself was to swallow my "ego," figuratively speaking.

As my dad rushed to get his clothes on, the thought that I was sick did not even occur to me. As we sped down Route 13, my parents kept trying to reassure me that everything was going to be alright.

Of course, I knew better. My mind had already been made up about what I had to do, though I could never get my parents to understand. Once at the psych hospital, things only started to get weirder. I thought that the people on the TV in the waiting room were laughing at and threatening me, saying I better not chicken out, or an eternity of pain awaited. As the intake was being completed, the delusion only became more real. The male nurse who did my intake had a goatee just like the one the devil is often depicted as having.

"Ok, you will see the psychiatrist, Dr. Evans, in the morning."

As they showed me to my room, my eyes darted back and forth, looking for something sharp I could use to commit the heinous act.

I was convinced that the entire staff at the psych hospital were really shape-shifting reptilians, and they were going to torture me until I had finished the job.

The hospital is not responsible for any objects lost or stolen, the sign on the bathroom mirror read.

How did I get myself in this position? I wondered. Had it really come to this?

I barely slept that night. In the morning, they served sausages and two hard boiled eggs for breakfast. Thinking the hospital staff were just fucking with me now by reminding me what I had to do, I gagged thinking about it and subsequently gave mine away.

During the morning check-in, all the patients came to the main room and sat in a circle to discuss how they were feeling. In addition to this, we all had to write a goal down on a sheet of paper of what we wanted to accomplish for the day. The fact that half of the patients were drugged up to the point of walking around like zombies, again, only made the delusion that I was in Hell more real.

"My goal for today is to get discharged out of here," I said, throwing up a hail Mary.

The staff eyed me; their gaze seemed shocked I had the gall to say that after "what I had done."

One staff member, Kareem, looked especially threatening.

"Don't worry, you'll get 'dis-charged' soon enough," his thoughts seemed to say.

After the meeting, I stole one of the pencils to take it to my bathroom, where I would attempt to do the dreadful deed. I then asked for hair clippers, saying it was to shave my beard.

There was no turning back now. I stabbed myself repeatedly for a total of seven times with the pencil, opening up the spongy tissue at the base of my phallus. The clippers were just sharp enough to cut away the skin in between the stab wounds I had made with the pencil. I shut off the clippers; it was too painful to continue. Kareem happened to be the staff member making rounds. Seeing the blood in my bathroom, he ran and got the nurse. They then numbed the area and stitched up the wound.

I remember being put on the eighth floor of the hospital after that until my wound had healed. They kept a member of the hospital staff with me at all times to make sure I didn't attempt anything again. I was convinced the staff were communicating with me through telepathy, and they were saying I had to finish the job.

C'mon, I thought. Hadn't I suffered enough?

Almost a week later, I returned to the behavioral health unit of the psychiatric ward. I noticed we all had to use crayons now at our morning meeting.

Of course, it was Kareem who was chosen to shadow me for the day. I remember I broke down crying after our morning meeting, dreading what was about to come next. Kareem sat next to me and tried to get me to pull myself together. In my mind I thought he already knew what I had to do.

"I want you to listen to me, Rohan."

I looked up at him with tears in my eyes.

"Always remember: God did not put fear in man."

Was he trying to help me? Were shape-shifting reptilians able to feel compassion?

The advice was exactly what I needed to hear to give it another try. This time, I would attempt to rip the stitches out while in the shower. Kareem was still the person shadowing me. I attempted to swallow the large knot in my throat as he followed closely behind me. Once it was just the two of us, I began my second attempt.

"Don't scream," his eyes seemed to say.

I tried repeatedly once again to mutilate my body, but after several attempts, I had to stop. It was just too painful. Kareem walked me out of the shower, still naked, to another one of the workers to show him what I had done. The swelling had become enormous, but after both of them took a look, they decided not enough damage had been done to alert the medical staff. They both gave me intimidating looks as I walked to my room with my head down.

Then an angel came down in the form of a roommate. His name was Brad, and we talked for hours on end. After hearing what I had done to myself, he read me passages in the Bible related to God's unconditional love and forgiveness. I was convinced Brad could read my thoughts, and with his help, I was able to rally back some self-confidence. I had made up my mind that I was not going to hurt myself ever again, and within a few weeks, I was discharged back to my parents' house. Although this was a dark chapter in my life, it taught me valuable lessons about how nothing I could ever do could stop God from loving me. It also helped me to love myself more unconditionally as well.

It's said that Man is only born with two fears: the fear of falling, and the fear of loud noises. All other fears are acquired throughout our life experiences. My therapist later told me that it took a lot of courage to attempt something like that, but the truth was it was the exact opposite. I was only doing it out of fear of even worse punishment I thought was to come. Looking back on it, it seems obvious my mind was playing tricks on me, but moving forward, I now had a scar as a very vivid reminder not to make decisions out of fear.

The Art of Self-Acceptance

"Because one believes in oneself, one doesn't try to convince others. Because one is content with oneself, one doesn't need others' approval. Because one accepts oneself, the whole world accepts him or her."

— *Lao Tzu*

The twenty-three months I spent at PICC forced me to grow in many ways. Many of the lessons I learned came not just from reading a multitude of self-help books, but actually interacting with other inmates. Being forced out of my element taught me how to deal with certain fears, as well as how to overcome the various challenges life can throw your way. It was by no means easy, but I came to terms with what I had done in my psychotic state and used what I had learned at my first job out of jail: becoming a spokesperson for NAMI. There, I became a young adult speaker for the "Ending the Silence" program where my team and I went into middle and high schools to speak to students about the importance of mental health.

Sharing my story with kids was therapeutic, and it also gave me a platform for which to share some of the wisdom I acquired in jail. I spoke about how important it was to express yourself and find an outlet for your negative emotions, rather than keeping them bottled up like I had done for years. By using my story as an example of what can happen when you remain silent about your issues, I felt like I was making a real difference for the first time in my life.

One of the most important lessons I learned on my path of self-growth came after I was released: how to accept yourself. Prior to being released, I had many periods in my life which I wished I could do over again such as the reckless behavior I displayed just before my manic episode, and the many occasions where I didn't speak up about the emotional pain I was going through until it was too late. But something occurred to me once I was freed from jail:

By regretting some of the poor decisions I made when I was younger, I was *invalidating* what I had been through. In other words, I was negating the path I had taken, as if it were a series of mistakes. Nonetheless, all these "blunders" were the same stepping stones I needed to become the person I am today; someone I can honestly say I am proud of. By invalidating my path, I was saying I wasn't accepting a part of myself.

Furthermore, by regretting bits and pieces of my past, as well as undermining the various challenges life had put before me, I was making it more probable I would do the same for future events as well. It was only when I began accepting myself as a whole that I truly began to love myself. Putting things in perspective and seeing the bigger picture, I began to see everything that came up in my life (good or bad) as more steppingstones to becoming the person I wanted to be. This included a brief period where I relapsed and started taking Xanax again.

My second year speaking to students as part of the "Ending the Silence" program became more difficult than the first. My confidence was down after a brief bout with depression I faced the previous summer, and to say I got off to a shaky start that school year would be an understatement. I struggled to get through the same presentation I had done a thousand times, as my fear of public speaking became obvious to all who watched. A particular speech I gave had me more rattled than usual, and even though I had my PowerPoint to refer back to, I just couldn't exude the same confidence I had so easily done the year prior. It was a tough crowd, and even though it was only a small group of students, the sound of laughter could be heard as I clicked through various slides. The next day, my team and I had to go back to the same school, and I couldn't face the fact I might get laughed at again. I caved into fear and stole a Xanax from a family member's prescription bottle before leaving the house.

I could feel the familiar rush of the benzodiazepine running through my system as I stood tall before the audience and delivered my speech. I had fun this time and it appeared the students enjoyed it as well, two of them coming up to me after and even asking for my autograph. I felt like a fraud, however, and was too ashamed to tell my supervisor what had caused the sudden improvement in my speaking.

Desperate to get my own supply, I asked my psychiatrist to write me a prescription of my own. She declined, as she knew my prior history of substance abuse. Determined to get my hands on more, I went behind her back and asked my general physician to write me a script, saying my anxiety was interfering with my work. He obliged, saying he would write me a script for thirty pills. When I went to pick up the script, however, there were sixty – along with a refill. With a hundred and twenty pills now at my disposal, it wasn't long before I began sliding back into my old patterns. I finished forty of them within the first two weeks, using them for even the mildest anxiety-provoking situation.

The effect on my self-esteem was different this time around, though. I began remembering what I had learned about invalidating myself through negatively judging my decisions, and instead of getting down on myself for relapsing, chose to define this as yet another steppingstone. Not only did this allow me to face myself in the mirror, but it gave me a chance to see how far I had come. I wasn't the same addict I was all those years ago. After coming to terms with my decision to refill my script, I found it a lot easier to use them responsibly. I also began rereading a book on overcoming stage fright, knowing that my prescription would soon run out and I needed a more permanent solution. Because I chose to define my actions as asking for help when I needed it, the effect I received back became exactly that. It was for this reason I would tell the students I presented in front of that I didn't regret anything that happened, and I was grateful for everything I had been through.

Finding Magnanimity

"There is neither happiness nor unhappiness in this world; there is only the comparison of one state with another. Only a man who has felt ultimate despair is capable of feeling ultimate bliss. It is necessary to have wished for death in order to know how good it is to live...the sum of all human wisdom will be contained in these two words: Wait and Hope."

— Alexander Dumas, *The Count of Monte Cristo*

During my time in jail, I read over sixty books with subjects ranging from Self-help, to Quantum Physics, Evolution, all the way to Dream Interpretation and Fiction. However, it was two autobiographies that I credit the most for allowing me to get through my sentence. One was "Long Walk to Freedom" by Nelson Mandela, and the other was "Man's Search For Meaning," by Victor Frankl.

To see what these two prominent figures had endured in their historic lives was almost unimaginable. Mandela, the more famous of the two, was sentenced to life in prison for fighting for equal rights in South Africa. He was eventually set free, but not before serving twenty-seven years under absolutely horrid conditions. Not only was he forced to perform hard labor under the most grueling circumstances, but he also faced torturous abuse from the prison guards on a daily basis. They tried everything from verbal abuse, to even urinating on him, yet they could not break his indomitable will. During his nearly three decades of incarceration under such brutal surroundings, he was able to write his autobiography "Long Walk to Freedom", using mostly toilet paper as his only means of documenting his struggles.

Victor Frankl's endeavor was even more horrific. In his book, he details his time spent in a Nazi concentration camp. For three years, he faced unimaginable savagery. Watching many of his fellow inmates, close friends, and even family (including his unborn child) die at the hands of the Nazi's, he noticed that it was the prisoners who managed to stay positive that survived. Like Mandela, he developed an indomitable will to live and even developed what is referred to as "logotherapy", one of the basic principles being that there is meaning under all circumstances, even the most miserable ones (hence the title of his book).

Anytime I even remotely felt sorry for myself for serving twenty-three months for something I felt was not fair, I drew strength from reading and re-reading these two brave men's stories. Even though I felt wronged by Drexel for expelling me, wronged by Dr. Amen for prescribing the wrong medication, and most of all wronged by the criminal justice system for putting a former medical student in the most violent jail in Philadelphia, how could I complain after learning of Mandela and Frankl's journeys through hell? At least in PICC I had access to food, a mattress, even a tiny window to look outside. I had a plethora of books to occupy my time, friends to laugh and joke around with, and despite all the violence I witnessed (and even experienced from time to time), it was incomparable to what these two resilient men had overcome.

By the end of my sentence, I had transformed into a completely new person; one who knew how to face life's challenges. It was for this reason I was able to forgive those toward whom I initially harbored much hatred. I had found countless ways how jail was the best thing to ever happen to me; ways I could never have imagined on that fateful day I signed the plea bargain the court offered me. Sure, there were dark times. And while there are still many areas I wish to grow in, I am no longer held back by anger and resentment. I had found forgiveness, not only for the various institutions which I felt acted unjustly towards me, but most importantly, towards myself. I had finally found magnanimity.

Epilogue

Upon receiving feedback for this book, one of the first criticisms I received was that it seemed like I went through this period alone and did not mention my family's help. I cannot stress enough the important role my family played in not only helping me get through those challenging circumstances, but also assisting me in getting this book out to you.

My mom, who visited me faithfully pretty much every Tuesday and Thursday, was the only one who I could count on to always pick up the phone when I called. Even when I vented to her the frustration of what I was going through, she took it all upon herself and listened, even when I yelled at her for what seemed like big things at the time, but of course, ended up being frivolous. The books she mailed to me while I was incarcerated were essential in my survival and were what allowed me to eventually thrive in jail. I cannot imagine the stress a mother would go through seeing her youngest son go off to jail, but I am who I am today because of her and because of what she did for me. She was the rock that provided me with a solid foundation in an otherwise turbulent time and for anyone thinking they could make it through such circumstances without such a person, I am telling you think again.

My dad not only paid my bail (the only reason I am alive to today) and my lawyer, but never lost faith in his son despite what I can only imagine were trying circumstances. Not everyone's father would pay those expenditures, but they were absolutely critical to my survival, and his lesson that "difficulties in life should   make you better, not bitter" was also vital for my success. I tried his patience many times during my recovery (and probably still do today) but without his love and support, I would have no success.

My brother's will and inner strength provided the framework which became my positive attitude today. I remember him telling me he almost failed out of medical school when all this was happening, and medical school can be difficult enough without having a brother incarcerated. But the fact that he finished and is a doctor today is a testament to his determination and I could not be prouder. I will never forget the time he took out of his unimaginably busy schedule to wait for hours in the visiting room just so he could see me, as well as the phone conversations we would have that uplifted my spirit when I needed it the most.

And last but not least, my good friend Prakash, who not only helped me get through my time when out on bail, but spent upwards of $500 on phone time. He might not have known it then, but there were times when the highlight of my day was our phone conversation.

Acknowledgments

A memoir such as this does not just happen as the result of one person. Sure, I may be the main character of the story (I hesitate to call myself the "hero", as there were many times I acted out of integrity) but it is the supporting cast who really made this book possible. Not just the actual writing and publishing, but in order to get this book to print I had to maintain my sanity at critical junctures, otherwise my story would remain in whispers about what was or what could have been. The following is an attempt to acknowledge those who helped me along the way, but is by no means a comprehensive list:

My mom, Ritu, father, Anil, brother, Rahul; Prakash Mallela, Sandy Kamel, Tianna Hansen, Laurie Pepe, Debbie Moritz, Nick Emeigh, Dave Piltz, Dr. Sophia, Dr. Vivian Shnaidman, Joe S, Parth K, Ed Quinn, Monku; Darryl Anka, Esther Hicks, and Alycia Pinkowski (RIP). Last, but not least, everyone who showed me love during what was an especially difficult time (including on State Road and beyond) and for those that continue to this day, my sincerest thanks.

About the Author

Rohan Sharma is a national speaker and rapper who goes by the stage name "Rx Mundi". He became an avid mental health advocate subsequent to serving a twenty-three-month jail sentence after pleading guilty to an armed robbery that took place in the fall of 2011. At the time, Rohan was a medical student at Drexel University. However, due to his mental illness being misdiagnosed, he was given the wrong medication, which induced a psychotic episode.

Rohan mainly speaks at high schools and college campuses as part of NAMI's "Ending the Silence" program, demonstrating the power of positive thinking to students as well as how he was able to create order in his life. His story has been featured by "This Is My Brave" – an organization dedicated to telling the stories of those afflicted with mental illness. In addition to this, he is being showcased in an upcoming documentary by academy award winning director Ken Burns.

About the Press

Rhythm & Bones Press is a small independent press in Pennsylvania dedicated to highlighting dynamic and inspirational authors whose work deserves to be acknowledged. They specialize in authors who write with personal emotion and those with trauma to portray to the world. They aim to help turn Trauma into Art. Visit *rhythmnbone.com* or find them on Twitter/FB @RhythmBonesLit or IG @RhythmBonesPress. Be sure to find this book on GoodReads and leave a review.

CPSIA information can be obtained
at www.ICGtesting.com
Printed in the USA
BVHW070129281019
562157BV00001BA/3/P